CHANGING THE GAME

Rewriting the Rules for Mid-Market Procurement

WILLIAM PEGG

CHANGING THE GAME
First published in Australia in 2017 by
Synthesis Group Pty Ltd
Queensland, Australia

National Library of Australia Cataloguing-in-Publication entry

Author:	Pegg, William, 1980 -
Title:	Changing the Game—Rewriting the Rules for Mid-Market Procurement / William Pegg
ISBN:	978-0-9944083-0-3 (pbk)
Subjects:	Industrial procurement
	Value analysis (Cost Control)
	Business enterprises (Finance)
	Strategic alliances (Business)
Dewey Number:	658.72

Author Photo by Jason Malouin
Cover design by The Scarlett Rugers Book Design Agency
Internal design by Gessert Books
Printed in Australia by Excite Print

Disclaimer
The material in this publication is of the nature of general comment only and does not represent professional advice. It is not intended to provide specific guidance for particular circumstances, and it should not be relied on as the basis for any decision to take action or not to take action on any matter which it covers. Readers should obtain specific professional advice where appropriate before making any such decision. Material referenced and the corresponding source locations are valid as at time of print.

PRAISE FOR CHANGING THE GAME

"William Pegg's book "Changing the Game" is a *tour de force* in reassessing the way we think about procurement. This is a practical guide, stuffed full with pearls of wisdom, about how to turn procurement, and hence cost management, into a source of cash flow and profitability. Well done William!"

Dr Andrew Walker Executive Chairman—Aspen Medical
2016 Australian Entrepreneur of the Year

"We live in a world that is all about doing business smarter. Every aspect of our business needs to be put under the microscope and rethought. That's where William Pegg comes in. He has taken the concept of procurement and turned it on its head. This is a very significant book for any company that has realised it has to do what it does differently and better. Thought leaders are found everywhere, William Pegg is one in the procurement space. Take his advice and your organisation will enjoy the benefits for many years to come."

Andrew Griffiths Business and Entrepreneurial Author
12 bestselling books sold in over 60 countries.

"Williams message is one that all business leaders need to know and understand—to be competitive in today's world we must elevate effective procurement principles to the forefront of business strategy. Get these principles right and you will not only improve profit, but increase innovation leading to greater top line performance. A great read, 'Changing the Game' is the companion guide for executive management and sales professionals alike, unlocking the powerful but often underutilised resource of our organisation's supply partners."

Eugene Visione Head of Sales and Marketing—Birch & Waite Foods

For Grace.

My closest companion and love of my life. We run this race together.

CONTENTS

INTRODUCTION

WHERE IT ALL BEGAN

It was May 2003, week one of my first job out of university. I had secured a fantastic graduate role with Unilever. My manager, Gary, an experienced professional who had a heart for training and grooming his team, told me: "Will, you won't be here for more than five years!"

As an impressionable 23-year-old, with nothing to my name except a university debt and a sky blue 1989 Peugeot 405, this left me lost for words. Had I tripped up in the dance of corporate politics, was my employer having second thoughts, was I the wrong fit?

At the time, I thought Gary had a screw loose. I was working for a progressive, people-conscious company—a company I still hold dear. It took me quite a while to appreciate the significance of that statement. Maybe it was Gary's understanding of the employment habits of young people at the time. Maybe it was an acknowledgement that the business would look to make redundancies over the coming years. Perhaps he saw my interest in something that was different to what large corporations can offer.

I remember very clearly a conversation we had around a year later. Gary put it to me: did I want to climb the corporate ladder or, in time, own my own business? I truthfully did not know. A remarkable display of generosity followed. Over the following years, Gary invested a considerable amount of time and energy to help me gain broad experience and exposure, which gave me the ability to make a choice and answer that question.

To this day, I am grateful for the candid advice and support provided at that early stage of my career. Advice that had no agenda or ulterior motive other than to see someone else succeed. I didn't know it then but those years at Unilever would have a significant impact on me professionally. It seeded in me the desire to educate business leaders in what is possible with the sole purpose of seeing their endeavours succeed.

Gary's comment was remarkably accurate. I stayed with Unilever a full five years and two months. From there, I worked in vertically integrated agribusiness and steel manufacturing. I provided consulting services to LNG oil and gas projects, and to a range of government departments and health care institutions. Working in strategic procurement, I was able to experience the good, the bad and the great by observing the process as well as people, company cultures, and industry trends.

I wouldn't trade that experience. It has been priceless. It is what has provided me with a rounded perspective. It's also what has given me a real passion for helping people, driving innovation and delivering a great 'fit-for-purpose' process.

WHAT I BELIEVE

Procurement can sometimes be seen as an inflexible, process-driven function that is not aligned with business operations, providing limited contribution to profit and growth. Yet it doesn't have to be this way.

Consulting may also be seen as an agent of pain rather than a contributor to gain. We have all met or heard of consultants who tell you things you already know, don't understand your business, fail to consider the medium to long-term impacts and tackle projects from a purely commercial mindset.

A rounded understanding of procurement, the aspirations of business, and how consulting can be improved brought about the formation of Synthesis Group.

As Australia's only firm that specialises in providing strategic procurement solutions to executive management of mid-sized companies, Synthesis Group is built with you in mind. You the leader or business owner, you the board member or you the executive manager.

We've got it all backwards. We put finance before people. In a world where people are looking for trust, rapport, leadership and innovation, we have to show that we can rise above self-interest. Clients and suppliers see through a one-eyed, what-ever-it-takes, commercial focus. This approach can disenfranchise and fragment business. No one likes to be treated as a commodity. Clients may look elsewhere, and suppliers may take their best thinking to your competitors. We cannot afford to let this happen.

Look at how Toyota works constructively with their suppliers or how Google and Virgin value their staff. The commercial focus is not ignored but enhanced, suppliers are not commodities but brought closer and valued, staff are not simply numbers but an integral part of the organisation.

Mid-market companies value agility, flexibility, and market responsiveness. Procurement can help by being strategic—by creating rapport and being innovative to deliver greater long-term commercial results. Procurement can contribute to a company's growth. It is in a position to improve top and bottom line performance. An outstanding strategic procurement function, one that intimately understands their business and what it values, will be able to craft flexible solutions that support the company's direction.

THIS BOOK

Large or small, every business buys goods and services. How a company chooses to manage and resource this 'buying' activity is varied so a clear and individual strategy is needed.

Changing the Game—Rewriting the Rules for Mid-Market Procurement is a transparent assessment of procurement. Its purpose is to take the knowledge and practices of successful big business and show how a change in procurement in mid-sized companies can generate greater financial returns.

Written for executive management of mid-market companies, this book addresses the question that many organisations ask:

"How can I make procurement a function that is flexible, supports company operations and helps my business profitably grow?"

I understand that some mid-market companies have procurement teams while others don't. Some organisations allocate the responsibilities of procurement throughout the business and others centralise it to a core team. While there are benefits to be gained from procurement activity originating from a single team, this book makes no recommendation on what is best. That is a decision for you.

No matter how procurement is currently performed, *Changing the Game* is written to give you the knowledge to improve the effectiveness of the current structure or create a new way of working. The goal of this book is simple—it is to equip you with the know-how so that procurement activity makes a greater contribution toward growth, partnership, innovation and profit.

THE MARROW IN THE BONE

My aim is to empower and educate. At the end of each chapter, there is a review of the key points that suggest how you can apply the changes directly to your business. There is also a self-assessment in the final chapter, allowing you to see in a single table how your company and procurement process measures up.

The book encourages you to convert newfound knowledge into a structured course of action. Most chapters contain interviews, case studies, and real-life examples. There are discussions with Origin Energy, Telstra, Unilever, Domino's, CSIRO and Woolworths. There are interviews with leading researchers and innovators, and stories that bring the content to life.

It has been a deliberate decision to interview and reference a selection of larger companies. The rationale is simple. Many big businesses are known for high performance in particular fields. By understanding how these successful companies work, you will be in a position to pick and choose the approach that is best for you. While the mechanics of their programs will probably be excessive for most mid-market companies, the principles that they apply will be relevant.

There is much to gain from improving procurement in your business, and it is my aim that this book will help you to achieve that growth and return.

PART 1

Framing Procurement

CHAPTER 1

A Framework for Success

FRAMEWORKS

We all have routines, ways of working that we follow each day for even the simplest of tasks and habits. Why do we do this? Humans are creatures of habit, and we like to follow a framework, a way of working that is familiar and effective.

The tasks we complete and our approach to interacting with others in our business dealings follow a path of our own mentally-mapped formula. This allows us to focus less on the 'what' to do and dedicate greater energies to the 'how' and 'why'.

To illustrate, I have a three-part method for preparing for meetings. I research the company, work to understand the people I am to meet, as well as note down their anticipated objectives. This helps me feel more comfortable and prepared.

No matter our process, we need to move from performing on autopilot to understanding what we do so we can refine it to improve future performance.

The best processes are those that are simple and easy to learn. If we struggle to outline what we do and why then it's probably unnecessarily complex. This invites inconsistency and the potential for error.

As the leader of your business, there are undoubtedly good reasons why you do things the way you do. You won't be alone if the mechanics, sequence and nuances of your process remain undocumented. To equip a team in high performance, this process—and the reasons for it—need to be clear.

To prevent it all coming apart at the seams, our processes need to be rigorous enough to cover the full scope of activities, and we need to demonstrate a willingness to change how we work when the circumstance demands it.

THE SHAPE OF STRATEGIC PROCUREMENT

What I have observed in procurement over many years is that no matter the industry, there are a number of principles that underscore companies and projects of high performance.

Strategic procurement is not technically difficult to learn. Many of the approaches are portable between industries and, if performed well, can deliver an increase in a company's profitability and growth. We need a framework to consistently fulfil that potential.

I apply a straightforward, five-part principle-based methodology. It is designed to create profitable, integrated, high-performance procurement.

These principles become the blueprint for all future activities and strategies. Incorporate these elements into your process and they will be a guide to help you create an exceptional way of working. These principles will help regardless of whether you are making decisions on the structure of the function, the composition of the team, its line of reporting, the allocation of targets or the breadth of responsibility for procurement.

1. INTEGRATION: WALKING IN THEIR SHOES

- What is the current state of operations?

- What does the desired outcome look like?

- How will every solution deliver the goals of the division and company?

These are the burning questions that procurement, or those responsible for the discipline, should be asking themselves and their stakeholders before an engagement begins. If you are unable to answer these questions, you're dead in the water.

It requires an understanding of the audience, knowledge of their dominant problems, the mistakes they make and what would frame an amazing solution. If procurement understands these details, if they are seen to be genuinely interested and engaged, then trust is built and opportunities for improvement begin to appear.

2. FLEXIBILITY: PEOPLE BEFORE PROCESS

An approach that I take in business is to ask 'What can I do for you?'

This is more than a question sales might ask a customer. It is a consideration of the needs of others before our own immediate interests. The purpose is to understand what our stakeholders want, so we can create effective solutions that resolve these needs.

Procurement as a function or a discipline needs to become less interested in textbook methodology and more focused on using knowledge to deliver flexible outcomes for stakeholders and business. Flexibility does not equate to a loss of rigour, nor does it imply cutting corners, rather a depth of knowledge that enables the delivery of outcomes that are valued.

3. PARTNERSHIP: THE OPPORTUNITY PLATFORM

Every business, even large multi-nationals that employ hundreds of thousands of people, only have access to a limited knowledge pool. The issue for mid-market companies is greater—fewer people, fewer resources.

Partnerships are crucial. Mid-market companies need those responsible for procurement to work collaboratively with internal colleagues, suppliers, industry bodies, universities, competitors and even unrelated industries to pool knowledge for an accelerated outcome.

They should be masters at brokering commercial and social agreements, engaging a varied audience as well as negotiating terms well beyond price. The skills needed to do this can and should be used to develop partnerships—the accelerant of commercial opportunities in our connected and digital world.

4. CAPABILITY: THE TALENT OF OUR PEOPLE

It is hard to produce something great if you only have average ingredients. The same is true for results in business. The quality of the procurement team has a direct correlation with the speed, uptake, effectiveness and financial outcomes experienced.

Is your procurement team performing at its peak? Are there opportunities to lift the standard and plug capability gaps? What about the talent of your supply and innovation partners—are they fulfilling all that you need?

In an age when transactional procurement roles are fast becoming obsolete, and only the strategic positions will survive, the capability of our people has never been more important.

5. COMMERCIALITY: CREATING LONG-TERM VIABILITY

Is procurement within your business focused on price or is total cost and value creation of greater importance?

The procurement process should consider the complete financial appraisal of a decision, extending well beyond the price paid. Does procurement in your business:

- Understand the complete supply chain and product cycle to spot areas for improvement
- Educate suppliers on how they can increase their efficiencies for your end advantage
- Improve back-end process that can erode front-end financial benefits
- Establish action plans to read, anticipate and respond to boom and bust cycles
- De-commoditise your inputs to limit the peaks and troughs of prices paid?

These five principles, when put into practice, will enable procurement to be more proactive, inclusive and commercially-minded.

COMMERCIAL TIE-BACK

Establishing a method, framework or set of principles provides guidelines for activities. This then becomes the standard and allows procurement to be performed consistently.

The framework creation process also presents an opportune moment to interweave a series of commercial 'gates' that need to be satisfied before a project progresses.

These metrics can be as varied and colourful as suits your organisation. Before a project is approved, it may need to demonstrate:

1. A single instance of innovation and the financial benefits from the concept.

2. How the affected internal stakeholders will be impacted positively and the financial consequences of the change.

3. How a minimum of 70% stakeholder engagement/adoption will be achieved and what the commercial consequences will be.

4. How risk has been reduced and how the commercial impact of the decision protects the company.

5. What process has been simplified. This may be shown by quantifying the commercial impact of shortening or accelerating an existing process.

TOP TIPS

1. Review the top three frameworks currently applied in your business.

2. Identify how these may be mapped out and adopted by your leadership team.

3. List the partnerships that your company has with other organisations. Are these effective? Investigate how they could be improved or what additional relationships could be sought.

CHAPTER 2

Six Common Mistakes

WHAT WE KNOW

Mid-market companies pride themselves on agility and responsiveness. They are large enough to out-compete SMEs and small enough to respond to market demand. Because they don't have crippling internal process, they often produce innovative solutions faster than their larger competitors.

These businesses run a tight ship when it comes to expense management and extracting value for money from the team and suppliers. It follows, every function needs to contribute to the bottom line. There is no ability to 'carry' underperforming teams or process. Unfortunately, procurement can find itself bundled into this category and retained only because someone has to buy the necessary goods and services.

Consequentially, mid-market organisations generally have lean procurement teams, structured in one of two ways:

1. A mid-level manager with oversight over a few transactional procurement positions or

2. Procurement becomes a secondary responsibility for a manager in finance, operations or project management.

We only know what we know. So if strategic procurement is not understood, then the above approach seems reasonable.

As Benjamin Disraeli, one of England's Prime Ministers in the 19th century, said: "To be conscious that you are ignorant is a great step to knowledge."

If procurement continues to be handled by mid-level management and transactional teams, then little of the potential available to business will be seen.

THE ARROGANCE OF IGNORANCE

Dr Ernesto Sirolli, an Italian entrepreneur and business coach, spoke at a TED Talk in 2012.[1] He described his experience as a young man working in Africa for an Italian NGO. The projects he was involved in dealt with technical cooperation with African countries from 1971-1977.

Sirolli described how his first project was to teach Zambian people horticultural practices. He and his team arrived in Southern Zambia where they were based in a beautiful valley that extended down to the Zambezi River. They brought with them a variety of seeds and set about the task of teaching the local people how to grow Italian tomatoes.

---

[1] TED Conferences 2012, *Ernesto Sirolli: What to help someone? Shut up and listen!*, viewed 25 April 2016,
https://www.ted.com/talks/ernesto_sirolli_want_to_help_someone_shut_up_and_listen?language=en

He described how, strangely to him, the locals had no interest in growing tomatoes—even the lure of paying them to learn had little effect.

He was amazed that the community lived in such a fertile valley and yet had no form of agriculture. As Sirolli described wryly—"thank goodness the Italians had arrived to save the Zambian people from certain starvation".

Everything flourished. Tomatoes grew to sizes that were twice as large as those grown in Italy, and Sirolli told the Zambians: "look how easy agriculture is."

When the tomatoes were red, ripe and the size of rockmelons, overnight 200 hippos came up out of the river and ate the lot!

Shocked and dismayed at the loss of his precious tomatoes, Sirolli was floored when the Zambians' simple response to the calamity was: "that's why we have no agriculture here."

In frustration, Sirolli asked why this key piece of information about hippos had not been shared, to which the Zambians' replied: "you never asked."

We tend to court the danger of assumption in business as well. We assume to know why things are the way they are and make plans based upon those assumptions. That is fine if you've got it right. More often than not, we have a less than complete picture and so our plans can terminally unravel.

MISTAKES APLENTY

Procurement, the function or the discipline, can and should contribute more to the bottom line. Unfortunately, in many businesses, there is a tendency for some to assume a complete understanding of procurement's capabilities, which can lead to it performing below its true potential.

Also, there are recurring challenges and mistakes made with regards to performance. Here are six common mistakes made by organisations when managing and working with procurement.

1. PROCUREMENT IS NOT SEEN AS STRATEGIC

In an environment where procurement only buys things and generates savings, is there little wonder that the function is not seen as strategic? Narrow mindsets produce a downward spiral in performance. It starts with a restriction of responsibility and then talented staff become harder to attract and retain. Without the right team, it becomes challenging to return value to the business, the executive's opinion of the function is validated, frustration creeps in and so the cycle continues.

THE WAY FORWARD

- Reconsider procurement's line of reporting—finance is not always the best fit. What does your business value most? What division is best placed to deliver these goals? The answer to these questions may determine where procurement should report and what targets it should adopt.

- Procurement needs to work closely with sales and marketing to understand the strategic business direction—new target markets, market share strategies and plans for new products. Armed with this knowledge, procurement can usher in appropriate suppliers for an introduction to sales and marketing for joint solution development.

- Procurement has a 'transferable skill set', enabling it to assist in areas traditionally off-limits. For instance, company-wide strategy planning, significant negotiations, strategic outsourcing, capital acquisitions and sensitive matters like dispute resolution.

2. INSUFFICIENT BUSINESS ENGAGEMENT

Procurement professionals can struggle to engage effectively with colleagues in business. In doing so, they run the risk of failing to understand business operations adequately. Dictating process from the safety of the 'ivory tower', procurement disengages and compounds any challenges through poor communication. This detached approach may be applied to suppliers as well, further exacerbating the problem.

THE WAY FORWARD

- Procurement needs to take the time to understand the stakeholder's business, their wants and needs and how 'value' is measured. Then, and only then, an approval board should allow procurement to develop solutions in consultation with the end-user.

- If you have a procurement team, consider embedding key members within a stakeholder's business to build trust, rapport and respect.

- When left on the bench there is little value to be offered. Instruct procurement to contribute toward marketing, sales, operations and finance meetings. Active participation brings a new perspective on well-worn ways of working.

3. QUESTIONABLE EFFECTIVENESS OF THE TEAM

Many organisations say staff are their most important asset. If this is so, why is it that procurement practitioners are all too regularly hired on industry experience alone, and in-house staff are given little or no training? While this situation prevails, procurement will struggle to deliver meaningful results.

Some people are not cut out for a role in strategic procurement. They appear to lack the commercial acumen, drive, interpersonal skills and the ability to deliver and communicate short and long-term project benefits. Then there are those in the profession who find it challenging to explain how an initiative contributes to company profit and growth objectives.

The best people will be found when HR and hiring managers understand what the procurement function can achieve and what skills, competencies, and experience are needed to deliver a great result. As I shared in an article for Human Resources Media (HRM Online), "HR has the opportunity to guide business in the selection of exceptional individuals—talent that breaks the convention of what procurement could and should do."[2]

THE WAY FORWARD

- Identify the aptitude, competencies and character traits required, and then look at skills and experience.

---

2 HRM Online, *Procurement: HR's secret weapon to commercial success*, viewed April 10 2016. http://www.hrmonline.com.au/section/featured/procurement-hrs-secret-weapon-to-commercial-success/

- Consider practitioners from outside your industry and the procurement profession. This allows access to different ways of working that may be new to your business.

- High-quality training can show a proactive, yet maybe inexperienced operator what is possible.

4. THE 'SAVINGS' FOCUS

There is a fixation in procurement circles on 'savings', unit cost reductions and cutting deals. While this is important, the reality is that the price paid for goods and services is only one cost of many. Sometimes, other internal costs of doing business are simply not considered.

A one-eyed 'savings' approach frequently produces a pattern of decline. Savings become harder to deliver year-on-year, and an increasing number of projects are required to deliver the same financial result. 'Lite' methodologies become commonplace. Supply relationships begin to deteriorate, stakeholders receive little to no support after program implementation, then, forecast savings figures are compromised due to minimal contract management. It doesn't have to be this way.

THE WAY FORWARD

- Encourage procurement to consider reductions in input costs beyond unit price. Examine alternative products, technology, and equipment for commercial and operational improvements. Assess internal process for duplication, bottlenecks and efficiency gains.

- Have your team review the 'Purchase-to-Pay' process. What efficiency gains are available in the generation of purchase orders through to the payment of invoices?

- If your business works closely with key suppliers, educate them on how to quantify, measure and reduce their internal input costs. Gains made here should be passed on to you.

5. SUPPLY RELATIONSHIPS ARE NOT VALUED

In some businesses, generating healthy supplier relationships can be seen as commercially irrelevant. If the only interaction with suppliers is to discuss price, the message being sent is that their goods and services are a commodity and the benefits they bring are of little value.

Like you, suppliers need to be profitable. If they are not, they won't do business with you for long. Exorbitant profits are not to be tolerated, yet it is important to agree fair and reasonable pricing.

Few suppliers will be willing to offer their best thinking when a relationship is only built around price. Innovation is stifled and instead of your business receiving their knowledge they take it to your competitors.

THE WAY FORWARD

- Build goodwill, you will need this in the lean times. Be open about your business plans, demonstrate the rewards for them by working equitably with you and deliberately work toward 'partnership', not 'vendorship'.

- Make yourself accessible. Suppliers that know executive leadership is available, consistently invest greater effort in delivering what is required.

- Create a culture of development and innovation. Incubators with suppliers are a great way to expedite the creation of new goods and services.

By working together, this approach has the effect of reducing supply cost but not necessarily the supplier's margin. This secures the savings and also the innovation. Always remember, if you don't work with your suppliers, your competitors will.

6. INADEQUATE FUTURE PROOFING

It is common for supply spend to be equivalent to 50 per cent to 70 per cent of a company's annual turnover. You would think this would be cause enough to consider how best to manage this expense. Too often businesses invest very little on how to future-proof and protect themselves.

Some companies don't have the appropriate programs in place to manage suppliers, control costs, and access innovation, and so they fall behind.

It is also common to see organisations without a structured means of identifying and mitigating risk. That line of thinking is fine, right up until an unplanned and significant disruption compromises the ability to operate.

THE WAY FORWARD

- Important suppliers need to be managed. Consider introducing a Supply Relationship Management program to address consistently innovation, price, quality and integration. This type of program flourishes when supported by executive management and when it receives input from the breadth of business—not just procurement.

- Develop crisis management plans that identify significant risk. Corrective actions are hammered out, the time to resolve is mapped, alternative supply locations are validated, and management responsibility is allocated. This allows for quick and decisive action to a significant and unplanned disruptive event.

- Category strategies can be considered. These are built to plan, manage and mature high-spend or critical supply options over the short and medium-term.

COMMERCIAL TIE-BACK

The notion of partnership and rapport is a theme that runs through this chapter and book.

Placing a 'hard dollar value' on partnership may be difficult to quantify. It's the subsequent business opportunities that result from the trust, collaboration and working strategically with suppliers and other businesses that bring about the most commercial gain. To illustrate this point:

- You may want to produce a new product. Your suppliers can contribute their technical know-how to make this happen.

- The profitability of a product or service needs to be increased. Your suppliers can work with you to find substitute inputs that reduce overall cost.

- A new market needs to be opened up. Supply and network partners can provide tips, advice, and those vital introductions to make this possible.

- You want to avoid buying through an agent. Your supplier can give you direct access.

- You need to buy ethically and sustainably, reduce your emissions footprint and improve your 'social licence' to operate. Once more it is your suppliers who are at the coalface to help make this possible.

Few of the above would be possible if there was no or only limited relationship in place. Yet each of these points has the potential to lift sales, reduce costs and/or ensure continuity of supply—all of which will have commercial implications for your business.

Partnership and rapport are the essences of future success and growth to which many companies aspire.

TOP TIPS

1. Review the prevailing opinion of procurement within your company and how it could be improved.

2. Identify which suppliers could and should be considered as collaborative partners and why.

3. Of the common mistakes outlined, in the table below, list which ones apply to your organisation and what plans can be created to reverse the effects of these mistakes.

Overcoming Common Mistakes

1. Procurement not seen as a strategic business partner

Current State:

Future Focus:

How to Close the Gap:

Financial Impact:

2. Insufficient business engagement

Current State:

Future Focus:

How to Close the Gap:

Financial Impact:

Overcoming Common Mistakes

3. Questionable effectiveness of the team

Current State:

Future Focus:

How to Close the Gap:

Financial Impact:

4. The savings focus

Current State:

Future Focus:

How to Close the Gap:

Financial Impact:

Overcoming Common Mistakes

5. Supply relationships not valued

Current State:

Future Focus:

How to Close the Gap:

Financial Impact:

6. Inadequate future proofing

Current State:

Future Focus:

How to Close the Gap:

Financial Impact:

PART 2

People and Relationships

CHAPTER 3

It Starts From the Top

As the leader of your business, you can empower and enable your team. Hopefully, this is not just because of your title but due to the respect that you have gained.

Outstanding procurement management is within reach. You can emphasise the importance of the broad skills required for an effective function, and you can lead divisional management to find the wherewithal that delivers the change.

PROCUREMENT LEADERSHIP

Procurement sometimes finds itself near the bottom of the corporate food chain. This may be due to a limited understanding of what is possible or the calibre and experience of the procurement team.

The success of procurement leadership in achieving business integration will increase if two factors are met. Firstly, executive management needs to support the procurement change program and be willing to go through a 'teething' stage to achieve improved results.

Secondly, procurement leadership has to have the ability to explore the business, warts and all. This can sometimes be painful and confronting but is often when hidden opportunities materialise.

Leadership promotes leadership. Executive management plays an important role in helping procurement achieve its potential. Supporting mid-management and the up-and-coming talent validates their role and builds them as individuals.

The growth in an individual's leadership ability can be illustrated by thinking of an ascending flight of stairs. Each step represents improvement and a more effective means of gaining traction.

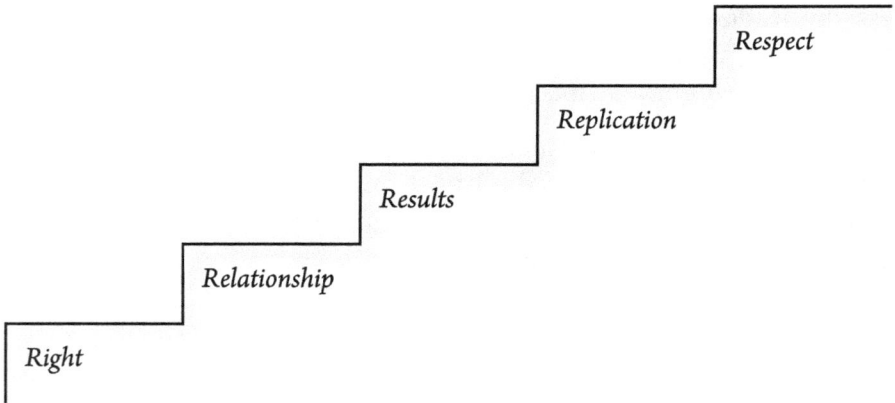

Ascending Leadership

1. **Right to Lead:** As a leader of your business, you have the authority to empower and appoint procurement with the 'right' to lead. This does not have to be complex and in many cases can be as simple as a new job title, a delivery target, open board-level support or increasing procurement's level of participation. The important point to note is that it takes one leader to empower

another. After this first step, it is largely up to those who have been tasked with the job to go and deliver it.

2. **Relationship:** The onus is now on procurement to develop relationships across the breadth and depth of the company, profession and supply base. Without relationships, without a level of genuine interaction, who will willingly follow?

3. **Results:** Proof is always in the pudding. Has procurement combined its knowledge and expertise with the relationships built, to deliver the required objectives? If results cannot be demonstrated, grand ideas and statements remain just that. This is a true test of leadership and knowledge, to be able to work through a challenge and deliver a well-timed result.

4. **Replication:** Procurement has kicked a goal and impressed the business leadership. Was it a one-off? Could it be done again? With the right approach to people, process and price there is every reason to believe the results can be replicated.

5. **Respect:** At this stage of the leadership cycle, management and operations should be confident (as should procurement) that a meaningful contribution can be made to advance the company's objectives. It is at this point that respect has been won. This may then be followed by larger, more significant opportunities to work collaboratively in business.

REACHING OUT

A man was at the beach, taking his son swimming in the breakers. A group of children were playing the game 'Over or Under'. As each wave was about to break, the call was made for the group to jump over or dive under.

A set of waves were forming further out and as they approached, it became clear that these were larger than the others. The first of the set loomed up in front of the group, and the shout 'Over' was called. The group jumped, and all seemed to clear the wave except for one girl. She jumped but was not quite able to clear the wave as it peaked, so was caught by the lip and thrown backwards.

The man saw the girl fall and noticed that she didn't resurface immediately. When she bobbed up, the excitement on her face from only a few seconds earlier was replaced with worry and concern as the second wave in the set bore down upon her, swallowing her in a wall of water. She remained under for a while and resurfaced coughing.

The young girl was now in trouble and the man began to move forward to help. That was when the third wave hit. Larger than the previous two, the girl was still coughing as it pummelled her into the sand. When she emerged, the fear in her eyes was clear.

By now, the girl was only a few strides from the man who immediately extended his hand and pulled her to shore. This man had a choice: watch the girl battle the waves alone or reach out and provide the help she so desperately needed.

The value of reaching out to those who may be struggling can never be underestimated. Executive management can transform the morale and results of a flagging team if focused assistance is provided. Assistance should always be offered without any agenda. Selfish ambition veiled as assistance will be recognised, often declined, and will only further compound internal challenges.

For someone who offers assistance freely and without strings, at face value it appears to cost them more than they stand to gain. The reality is that benevolent behaviour regularly attracts positive consequences. In the context of business, this may include improvement in performance, higher retention of staff, increased workforce satisfaction and securing 'allies' who can remain favourably inclined years into the future—often well beyond employment with your business.

There have been two leaders that I've worked with early in my career whose actions will remain with me all my life. These individuals took the time to develop and expose me to senior leadership that I would otherwise have been unlikely to encounter on my own. They guided me through the corporate minefield with no other agenda but to see me succeed.

I will always be grateful for their selfless help. I have and will continue to be compelled and delighted to do whatever I can to help these wonderful individuals.

If procurement is underperforming and could use some assistance, I encourage you to integrate the function into the lifeblood of your business. Grant them the licence to dig into the details. Then explain the ascending leadership model and reach out to assist if they are struggling for air. You may be surprised where this takes you.

IT STARTS WITH TALENT

You can have the best systems, process, technology and operations, but if your people are not cutting the mustard, then you will frequently fall short.

Visna Lampasi, General Manager Group Procurement at Woolworths Limited, shared her perspective on the importance of investing in and grooming talent.

I first met Visna in 2009 when working in heavy industry, and since then have observed and experienced first-hand her genuine belief in the need to shape the future of procurement by enhancing the calibre of talented, up-and-coming professionals. So it came as no surprise when she talked about a new procurement-specific graduate program launched within Woolworths in 2015.

The three-year program selects the brightest talent from the annual Woolworths graduate intake and aims to expose capable individuals to the full breadth of procurement functionality across its six departments. As a company with 205,000 employees and an annual turnover in FY2016 of more than AUD$58 billion, it is hardly surprising that there is a need for specific departments within procurement.[1]

The first two years of the program unwraps the extent of what is possible within procurement. These years demonstrate how the function can contribute towards the organisation's strategic objectives and financial targets. However, it is the third and final year of the program that is most interesting. Only high performance, high potential graduates are 'invited' to participate.

The first six months has the graduates shadowing Visna throughout the business and working on the most strategic of initiatives including new business development, mergers & acquisitions, minority supplier development, ethical & sustainable sourcing and innovation.

The last six months of the program is an offshore posting. Graduates work with the international sourcing team and help develop quality supply chains and products for export back to Australia and New Zealand.

Not all companies have the means to put in place a program of this scale, nor would it necessarily be appropriate for most mid-market organisations. Nevertheless, there are a number of principles that can be drawn out here:

---

1   Woolworths 2016, *Woolworths Group Annual Report 2016*, viewed 30 October 2016, http://www.woolworthsgroup.com.au/icms_docs/185865_annual-report-2016.pdf

1. **Groom your young talent.** Gen Y and Millennials enjoy change, challenge, and exposure. It is not always about the size of the remuneration package but how it is structured, the opportunities and how they are engaged. If we can demonstrate a willingness to identify and work with this upcoming group, then there is a higher likelihood of improved output and workforce stability.

2. **Time and attention.** It pays dividends for senior leadership to invest time and interest in the development of a select few. This investment is not lost on talented individuals and so helps frame their approach to management when their time comes.

3. **The selfless leader.** Generational thinking is required for the grooming of future leaders. It moves beyond what you can gain for immediate personal interests and focuses instead on the legacy you can leave through the education and empowerment of others.

WHERE THE TALENT HIDES

Procurement is not a difficult discipline. Whilst you need knowledge of what makes a great process to deliver exceptional results, a bright individual who is offered the correct training and management support can learn it with relative ease.

Unlike a lawyer, pharmacist, accountant or even ecologist who require professional qualifications to practice, in the past, the professional prerequisite for procurement has been a backside on a seat. This is beginning to change with more universities offering undergraduate and post-graduate programs in supply chain and procurement. The makings of a great procurement operator are not so much in their technical skills (tendering, contracts, risk management, and supplier performance) but the extent of their interpersonal abilities, commercial acumen, and rounded business experience.

Technical skills are not redundant; rather, commercial acumen and the ability to engage and relate with others are of greater importance. Technical skills can be learned—aptitude along with the ability and willingness to effectively engage are largely innate. When talking to recruiters and hiring managers, it is not uncommon to hear that there are few talented procurement professionals in the market and that fewer are actively looking for work.

Highly-specialised jobs will always require highly-trained people. For roles that do require extensive years of experience, it is important that those members of the procurement team have outstanding knowledge.

Yet most procurement roles are not technically demanding. If this is the case for your business, your ideal candidate may not need years of procurement or even industry experience. Companies may well be hunting for talent in all the wrong places.

Many professionals, myself included, 'fell into' the profession. My university background was biological sciences. I graduated when employment in environmental science was just not popular, and I couldn't find work. I made the switch to business and have been there, and revelled in it, since.

This unplanned landing in procurement has been possible due to low barriers to academic entry and the range of roles available from trans-actional through to strategic—yet the function is frequently assessed through that single transactional lens.

If the 'drought' of quality procurement practitioners arises from us looking in only one small conventional talent pool and if the skills required to perform the job effectively can be taught without too much fuss, where exactly should we be looking?

Sales, science and manufacturing are professions with rich pickings.

Polished sales professionals understand how to balance commercial drivers with rapport. Both of these elements are essential to procurement. Procurement has to 'sell' every day—sell the merits of a change to stakeholders, sell the importance of constant improvements to suppliers and sell the need for support and sponsorship from management.

Those with a background in science are taught to have an analytical and enquiring mind that constantly questions and critiques. Procurement is not a function for fence sitters. You are either engaged in the business, agitating for constructive change, or you're not. It is that simple.

Manufacturing industry experience is another invaluable avenue. While this has been in decline in Australia over recent decades, professionals from this industry bring highly valuable insights. These individuals usually have a thorough understanding of supply chains, know-how to consider multiple moving parts and inputs, and they appreciate the importance of innovation, efficiencies in process and continual improvement.

Of course, there will be other possible talent sources such as finance and operations, some of which may be more suited to your business and profession. What I would like to do is plant the thought that there are other avenues that may produce better results than the well-ploughed fields of the past.

QUESTIONS FOR CANDIDATES

A claim that we've all heard is that people are a company's greatest resource. Ask yourself, does your business have the best resource to carry out procurement?

Securing great people can be a challenge. If management in mid-market firms has a limited view of what is possible, it is probable that the most instructive interview questions will be missed.

Over the following pages are a series of questions that should be considered when selecting competent personnel. Give this list to your management team to help get the process under way.

This list is not exhaustive. What these questions will do is help you assess the experience, competencies, skills and abilities of a candidate against what is needed for a role in procurement. And remember, attributes are going to vary with the seniority and technical demands required.

Whether a candidate has procurement experience or not, there are a number of broad questions that can and should be asked. Try the following:

Questions for Candidates

Question	Intent
1. Outline your experience in 'selling' a concept or change program. What audiences have you had to engage and sell to? How did you do this and what were the results?	Procurement is frequently non-mandated and operates in challenging environments, so it's important to have the ability to pitch and 'sell' a program for it to gain traction.
2. For the following options, select the three you believe to be most important and explain your answer: commercial gains, innovation, supplier rapport, technology, partnership, communication skills, and savings.	This provides insights into what the candidate values most and why. Your business will have a particular focus. Therefore, it's important to match the drive of candidates with the company's direction.
3. Scenario: you have a situation where there is internal resistance to a new program. You require executive-level sponsorship, need a reluctant supplier to become proactively engaged and have to overcome internal resistance. How would you go about achieving this?	Managing problems and resistance to change is a requirement for procurement. How an individual goes about these potentially challenging tasks tells a lot about their character and interpersonal skills.
4. Describe how you would go about developing constructive long-term relationships within your business and with external stakeholders. Provide an example from your working experience.	The candidate's ability to develop partnerships and rapport is being examined here. Both are essential requirements for success in procurement.

Question	Intent
5. What would be your approach to understanding a company's various internal business units? How would you effectively integrate with them?	Procurement must be able to integrate. To be effective requires a thorough understanding of certain parts of the business. A selfless approach to working with stakeholders is needed.
6. Provide an example of how a project you have delivered has directly improved the company's financial performance.	Whether it hits the top or bottom line, every activity or project must have strong commercial merits. This question is designed to identify if the candidate understands this need.
7. What is more important to you—leading edge process or flexible process? Explain your answer.	Business may not necessarily be concerned with the mechanics of procurement (assuming it is legal, professional, ethical and sustainable) but rather their level of consultation and the end result. Leading process may actually be a backward step for a mid-market company. Instead, flexibility should be encouraged.

COMMERCIAL TIE-BACK

Why are consultants brought into a business? It's not because they are less expensive in the short term. The answer (hopefully) is that they have broader experience, can deliver a faster turnaround with improved commercial results and that they bring specific skills not found in your company.

So if any of these reasons resonate, let me ask another question. Why don't you hire staff for the procurement function with broader industry or professional experience, who can deliver an improved result with a faster turnaround because they have skills not currently found within your company?

Look for talent beyond the conventional hunting grounds and, more than likely, these fresh eyes will deliver commercial and operational returns beyond what you have experienced in the past.

TOP TIPS

1. How has procurement leadership in your business been empowered for success?

2. Consider how additional support could be offered to encourage greater results.

3. Where does your business conventionally source procurement talent? Consider what improvements could be brought through the introduction of alternative capabilities.

CHAPTER 4

Profiling Procurement

An anecdotal opinion in industry is that there is something different, possibly unusual about the procurement profession. It may be interesting to learn that those in the profession speak about the challenges engaging stakeholders and securing project adoption. Both these opinions have a valid foundation.

Dr Sara Cullen is an internationally-renowned advisor, author, and strategic contracts expert. She is the managing director of The Cullen Group and is a research fellow at the University of Melbourne, Australia.

For some years now, Sara has been conducting research into the management styles of procurement professionals in the public ('government') and private ('commercial') sectors.[1] In discussion with Sara, she shared how these management styles for procurement vary between the two sectors and also differ from that of internal stakeholders and suppliers. This is a crucial piece of work as it helps explain procurement behaviours and importantly, aids in candidate profiling.

---

1 Research is ongoing and so remains unpublished. Dr Sara Cullen provided live data for direct purposes of publication within Changing the Game.

Dr Cullen's study began in 2011 and is ongoing. Building on her previously published findings[2] [3], Sara shared her results as at July 2016. At that time, around 1,900 individuals had contributed, more than 1,250 in Australia alone.

Participants are asked forty-five questions. The responses are collated and the individual is classified into one of six management styles.

The Six Management Styles

Management Style	Management Characteristics
Relationship Developer	Facilitator of trust, respect and interpersonal relationships.
Problem Solver	Makes things happen, overcomes roadblocks and breaks barriers.
Organiser	Maintains records, audit trails, controls and plans processes.
Entrepreneur	Seeker of innovation, better ways of doing things and long-term potential.
Scanner	A networked/connected individual, a natural explorer and benchmarker.
Monitor/Protector	Ensures the organisation is protected, risks are addressed, and compliance is comprehensive.

---

2 Cullen, S. (2012). A study of contract management styles in Australia 2011-12. https://www.cips.org/Documents/CIPSAWhitePapers/2012/A%20study%20of%20contract%20management%20styles%20in%20Australia%202011-12.pdf

3 Cullen, S., Lacity, M. and Willcocks, L. (2014) *Outsourcing: All You Need to Know*. White Plume Publishing, Melbourne.

Figure 1 shows Dr Cullen's lead styles in action—430 Australian procurement participants, 259 in commercial and 171 in government. The lead style, or most commonly identified management profile for procurement, is Relationship Development (31% of respondents) for the commercial sector and Organiser (32%) for the government sector.

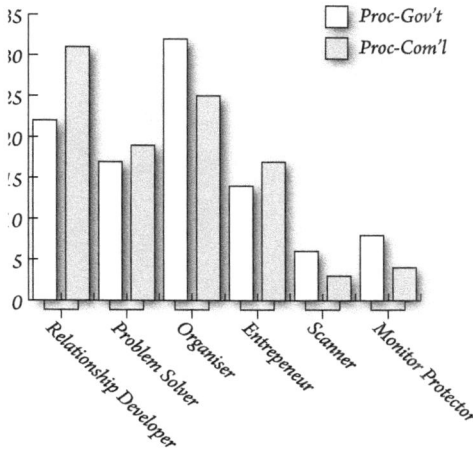

Figure 1: Lead Style for Procurement—By Sector

While the dominance of these sector-specific lead styles should come as little surprise, what is interesting to note is that both of these lead styles also carry the greatest difference between the sectors. Developing relationships is valued significantly more in the commercial sector while being an organiser is of greater value to government.

The data was then cut a different way. Figure 2 compares the lead styles in the commercial sector for procurement, their stakeholders, and suppliers. Two compelling findings emerge.

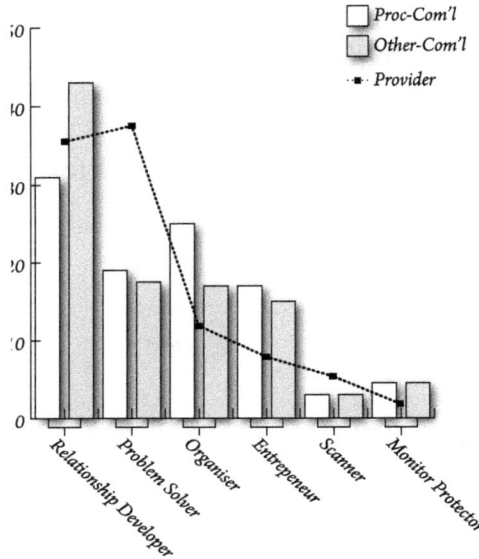

Figure 2: Lead Styles of Commercial
Sector

Finding 1: When a comparison is made between the three groups, what is immediately obvious is that the procurement function has less focus on relationships than that of internal stakeholders and suppliers. Procurement instead appears to be more concerned about process and control mechanisms.

While 31 per cent of procurement respondents believed that Relationship Developer is of most importance, a comprehensive 43 per cent of internal stakeholders believe this to be true. In other words, almost half of the non-procurement people in business believe relationships are the most important management style compared to only one-third of those in procurement. In contrast, the second strongest lead style for procurement was Organiser at 25 per cent of respondents, yet only 17 per cent of procurement's stakeholders believed this to be an important lead style.

Procurement does not value professional rapport enough, and business does not think much of procurement's fixation on process, maintaining records, audit trails and controls.

Finding 2: For procurement's two strongest lead styles (Relationship Developer and Organiser), suppliers are more closely aligned with internal stakeholders than they are with procurement. As Sara says, these results help explain why it's common for procurement to feel that suppliers and procurement's own internal stakeholders are conspiring against them. This is not necessarily the case—it is just that the two groups are more aligned to relationships rather than organising.

WHERE TO FROM HERE

As the saying goes, perception is reality. Maybe in procurement's case, reality is reality. Procurement's apparent inability to value relationships as highly as its colleagues and its focus on process and controls will only frustrate business, not empower it.

Two options are available to executive management: train the current team or recruit a different type of procurement professional. Both options are possible, and both have their limitations.

Chapter 3 addressed the means for finding capable individuals from outside the conventional talent pool. But what about training?

TRAINING

We have all been on training courses where much of the content is forgotten within two weeks. Whether the course is public or private, it's important for a program to encourage participants to identify projects that can be implemented immediately.

Training is not an information dump and run exercise. I like to lift the effectiveness of training by providing post-event troubleshooting webinars to deal with any of the implementation issues that may arise. The great thing about this approach is that it allows me to work alongside a company and walk that journey of growth with them.

For those who think training is a waste of money, consider the following:

Two business leaders were discussing the calibre of their team. One executive suggests the approach of training the team to overcome the knowledge gaps. The other executive replied, "It's a waste of money. Besides, if we train the team they might then leave." To which the other replied, "If we don't train them they might just stay!"

COMMERCIAL TIE-BACK

Dr Cullen's research showed that nearly 50 per cent of the staff in functions other than procurement believed that developing relationships was the most important management style. The second closest management style was 'Problem Solver' and that had support from less than 20 per cent of respondents.

So what does this mean? One way of looking at it is that procurement personnel may be deficient in interpersonal skills. The other and more probable implication is that there is something in the notion of rapport-based commercial interaction after all.

If a significant proportion of internal stakeholders and suppliers value relationships and if procurement was able to place a similar level of value on this lead management style, then imagine the possibilities:

- Contracts would reward high supplier performance that benefits your business, not simply penalise them for faults.

- Suppliers would be more open with their books and work collaboratively in minimising expense rather than fearing an attack on margins.

- Internal stakeholders would be heard, valued and understood, resulting in accurate, effective and flexible procurement solutions being built with greater internal adoption.

- New technology and capital investment would be willingly brought to your 'table' before your competition allowing you to create new products and release them to market first.

Rapport-based commercial interaction is not just a feel-good concept but a robust, expense reducing, profit earning strategy.

TOP TIPS

1. Review whether procurement values relationships and rapport as highly as the rest of your business. Investigate how a culture of rapport-based commercial interaction can be encouraged and adopted by procurement.

2. Review whether your procurement department has a heavy fixation on process, control and records. Consider what alternative outcomes could be achieved if procurement had a greater focus on results over process and flexibility over rigidity.

3. Consider what would deliver the greater and faster return to your business—training the current team or seeking talent from a different source.

CHAPTER 5

Why Bother With Rapport

THE SOCIETY WE LIVE IN

Much of what we purchase today doesn't last. We have been conditioned to expect this. You might get a few years of life from your television, far less than the old rear-projection cathode ray types. Your laptop and phone will become obsolete within two years, electronic devices don't seem to go the distance any more.

A friend of mine owns a lovely sports car. It looks and sounds great but it's just a little sensitive. On the third instance of having to call out roadside assistance, the mechanic's comment said it all: "These cars are not built to last."

How we take care of our relationships isn't much better. According to the Australian Bureau of Statistics (ABS), in 2014 around 121,000 marriages were registered.[1] Around 33,000 or 28 per cent of those marriages involved one or both people marrying for at least the second time. For that same year, 46,500 divorces were granted. Without considering how long a marriage lasts (although ABS claims the median

---

1 Australian Bureau of Statistics 2016, *Marriages and Divorces, Australia, 2014*, cat. no. *3310.0*, *ABS*, *Canberra*.

to be around 12 years), these raw numbers suggest that the equivalent of almost 30 per cent of registered marriages end in divorce.

What has become evident is that we live in a society that is quite comfortable with the temporary nature of what we own and the willingness to buy, replace, recycle, upgrade. We live in a society that is highly accustomed to the disposable nature of goods and relationships.

While so much of what we own is not built to last and can easily be replaced with an affordable alternative, our own personal relationships are subject to high rates of failure too.

This attitude can be expressed with equal strength in business as well. Too often the relationships that we aim to cultivate with clients and suppliers are approached from the perspective: 'what's in it for me?'

I'm not suggesting a business relationship with a supplier or collaborative partner be permanent. We are however at risk of the pendulum swinging too far the other way. What becomes apparent is the accepted attitude that some of us have toward the disposing of business relationships. Rapport and mid-term commercial opportunity are sacrificed for the short-term deal. This is an attitude that has been built into our subconscious, often from a young age, since after all if it does not work, toss it out.

It is vital that we conduct the necessary due diligence, make wise decisions and ensure business relationships are profitable. We also need to stop, draw breath and think if we could achieve more through a desire for constructive, commercially healthy, progressive partnerships.

SETTING THE BAR

As automakers go, Toyota is the world's largest seller. It is larger than General Motors and, as Richard Levick from *Forbes Magazine* explained in a 2013 article, that's no mean feat, especially since from 2009, the company had been under intense public scrutiny surrounding unintended acceleration investigations, recalls, and litigation.[2]

As a Japan-based auto firm, Toyota largely 'outsources' vehicle production to U.S. suppliers. It has had significant operating facilities in the U.S. since the mid-1980s, employing approximately 40,000 Americans. Consequentially, Toyota has grasped the importance of bridging the cultural divide so often present with companies that choose to move offshore.

Toyota has around 500 key suppliers in North America. It tightly controls design and engineering and continues to build strong relationships with those suppliers who consistently show the ability to deliver on time, maintain quality, control costs and innovate.

Levick goes on to say that this supply network is characterised by a high degree of trust, with rewards for timely delivery instead of just penalties for delay. This results in the fastest production and assembly times in the auto industry, consistently high quality and yet still with the ability to deliver commercial savings.

Granted, Toyota is a huge company, 8th largest globally when ranked by revenue according to a 2015 Global 500 study performed by *Fortune Magazine*.[3] The fact that it is so large is what makes its approach with suppliers so much more remarkable.

---

2 Levick, R 2013, 'Spotlight on Outsourcing: Boeing Scrambles as Toyota Triumphs', *Forbes*, 30 January, viewed 25 April 2016,
http://www.forbes.com/sites/richardlevick/2013/01/30/spotlight-on-outsourcing-boeing-scrambles-as-toyota-triumphs/#28f6c052345c.

3 Fortune 2015, *Global 500*, viewed 25 April 2016,
http://fortune.com/global500/

ELASTIC RAPPORT

What ability exists in your business for procurement to establish, grow, strengthen then relay forward a relationship with a supplier so that other parts of the business can continue to work effectively? I'll call this 'elastic' rapport.

One of procurement's operational goals should be the creation of 'elastic' relationships. That is, the ability to transfer to internal stakeholders a healthy and functioning relationship developed between the supplier and your business.

A supply relationship forced upon a business without consultation, particularly for high-spend or highly critical goods and services, is not a great way to start. It's a bit like being told as a youngster whom you should date and then being made to go along with it, even if your heart's not in it.

Business relationships are just that—relationships. They can come and go but the great ones last. Procurement playing 'cupid' without consultation is destined to be a rough path.

Engaging the affected business functions from the outset is very important. What are their challenges, where do the opportunities lie, what mistakes have been made previously? And what opinions are held of the various supply solutions; what's stopped this change being made before?

These are just a few of the questions procurement should be asking stakeholders who may have a vested interest in a change program. Involving the business before an activity commences demonstrates forward-thinking rapport as well as common courtesy and respect. It is amazing how something so simple can go such a long way.

Keep in mind that once a market activity has been completed, once the contract is signed and the need to return to business as usual looms, the supplier must be able to work with the stakeholders. After the dust has settled and procurement returns to an overarching management role, it's how the two parties interact without procurement that will be the key to longevity and success.

Always remember that the vast majority of suppliers want to work with your business and will go to great lengths to make this possible. Developing elastic rapport is a rock-solid means of successfully achieving this collaborative objective.

A MEASURED APPROACH

Now before we get too carried away with the idea of great supplier relationships, I need to emphasise the importance of a balanced approach. As John Harney, the Chief Procurement Officer from Domino's Pizza describes it, we need to have a 'three-legged milking stool', consisting of commerciality, innovation, and relationship.

As rapport without commercial rigor and innovation would fail to deliver sustained solutions, so too would commercial rigor and innovation without their respective bedfellows.

As with all activities in business, simplicity is best. Have a planned, logical approach for managing rapport with suppliers:

1. Choose your supply partners carefully. Establish selection criteria that identify only those companies that complement your targeted direction.

2. An agreed management and appraisal structure will help the relationship progress through all seasons and business cycles.

3. Be specific about how each identified supplier can contribute to your business growth and what the opportunity will be for them.

I remember speaking at a conference in Sydney. It was for a pharmaceuticals association, and I had been asked to discuss a strategic approach to outsourcing.

The last of my slides provided an overview of what success looks like with well-run strategic partnerships. Acknowledging that we are not talking about outsourcing, a number of takeaways from that presentation are highly applicable for what we are discussing here.

1. **Document your process and IP:** Insulate yourself from risk by recording all process, practice, understandings, and IP. That way, if a key team member leaves, the supplier relationship will not suffer.

2. **Be accountable:** Make sure both your business and your supplier clearly understand what is required and from whom. Remember to own both your success and setbacks.

3. **Develop partnerships and trust:** Position talented staff to manage the arrangement. Be prepared to visit your supply partner. Develop relationships and don't play the 'blame game.' You want them to know you are a long-term partner, not just a fair-weather friend.

4. **Anticipate teething issues:** As with all relationships, enter the agreement with a high level of patience. Have a risk register on-hand with pre-established remedial actions.

5. **Metrics:** Have a set of measures that test the 'temperature' and effectiveness of the business relationship. This may revolve around innovations introduced, simplification of process, commercial improvements and/or how interaction is performed.

CASE STUDY: SUPPLIER COLLABORATION

In May 2013, Oxfam released its report *Standing on the Sidelines* that identified the 10 most significant greenhouse gas (GHG) emitters in the food industry.[4] Two of the 10 companies named included General Mills and Kellogg.

Both General Mills and Kellogg responded to the report in similar ways. The online food publication, BakeryandSnacks.com, reported in August 2014 that both organisations had pledged to disclose their GHG emission targets by December 2015.[5] They would also reveal their top three suppliers of palm oil, soy, and sugar cane and achieve zero deforestation in high-risk supply chains by 2020.

Kellogg went one step further in its pledge by asking key suppliers to measure and publicly disclose their emissions and reduction targets.

It is one thing to make such requests of the supply base; it's a whole other matter to deliver them successfully. To achieve this, a shift in how the suppliers are engaged would no doubt be required.

I spoke with BakeryandSnacks.com in August 2014 about possible means for General Mills and Kellogg to deliver on these environmental pledges.[6] Some approaches included the development of systems, tools and process for suppliers, which could deliver both a greater

---

4 Oxfam 2014, *Standing on the Sidelines—why food and beverage companies must do more to tackle climate change*, 186 Oxfam Briefing Paper, Oxfam GB for Oxfam International.
https://www.oxfam.org/sites/www.oxfam.org/files/bp186-standing-sidelines-big10-climate-emissions-200514-en_2.pdf

5 Culliney, K, 2014, 'Oxfam: Kellogg rises above General Mills on climate change', *Bakeryand-Snacks.com*, 13 August, viewed 20 June 2015
http://www.bakeryandsnacks.com/Manufacturers/Kellogg-climate-change-policy-ahead-of-General-Mills-says-Oxfam

6 Culliney, K, 2014, 'Actioning environmental pledges: Strategic engagement with suppliers critical, says procurement expert', *BakeryandSnacks.com*, 20 August, viewed 20 June 2015,
http://www.bakeryandsnacks.com/Commodities/Environmental-pledges-need-strategic-supplier-engagement.

likelihood of program adoption and a greater consistency of data. Another consideration was the need to provide boots on the ground to assist with education and implementation, ensuring systems did not replace rapport.

Whether it be the reduction in carbon emissions, the determination of local content in your goods and services or any other program that requires considerable supplier input, there are several issues that are important to remember:

1. Recognise that there will be varying levels of awareness and acceptance on some topics.

2. Supplier education and training may be required to help you achieve your objective.

3. Placing activities in the hands of your suppliers does not absolve your company of responsibility—particularly in the court of public opinion.

4. Demonstrate that you have skin in the game too.

This example helps illustrate the benefits of developing strategic supplier relationships. A commoditised supplier may present resistance to working on such an involved program. A supply partner, a company that sees the commercial and strategic advantages of collaboration, will be far more willing to engage and invest time and resources in assisting with your internal objectives.

The underlying message here is a need to build and leverage strong supply relationships. Strong relationships and a willingness to work together could—in the case of General Mills and Kellogg—result in GHG reductions and an improvement in their social licence to operate.

COMMERCIAL TIE-BACK

At first glance, a focus on developing rapport with selected suppliers may seem to have no or only limited commercial advantages. When you take the time to examine how other successful businesses operate, you see that collaboration is a regular way of working.

Novel engineering solutions through a continual improvement mindset are one of the positive consequences of developing supplier rapport.

I worked with a vertically integrated agribusiness company in Australia where part of its operations involved cold food processing and value-add manufacturing. Material handling (forklifts) were an integral part of these operations but were subject to a high degree of wear and tear due to the wet and cold operating environment.

For this business, repair and maintenance costs had been on the rise. A strategic relationship had been developed with a material handling supplier who consequentially brought these increasing maintenance costs to the attention of their client. The supplier offered to perform, at no cost, an audit and assessment to identify causality, trends and remedial actions.

The work revealed units in a particular part of the plant had higher servicing needs due to the constant presence of water and that consequentially, non-stainless bearings failed fast. An alternate stainless steel bearing was sourced, trialled and found to be effective. Not only did maintenance costs decrease but the alternative corrosion-resistant product was supplied at a lower price.

The project saved just that one facility more than AUD$200,000 a year and was rolled out across a number of other facilities that were experiencing similar challenges.

Without the prior development of constructive rapport and partnership, it would have been highly unlikely that the supplier would volunteer—at their expense—to explore, research and rectify this issue that until that point had gone unnoticed.

TOP TIPS

1. Identify the innovative gains that have been brought to your organisation through constructive supplier relationships. Investigate other focus areas of growth and innovation and how your suppliers can contribute.

2. In the table below, list the areas of greatest challenge or criticality within your business. Identify which suppliers (incumbent or otherwise) operate in this space. Think how your business could work more collaboratively to resolve these pinch points.

3. Identify the selection and management criteria that would be most appropriate for your business to develop strategic partnerships with your key suppliers.

The Areas of Greatest Challenge

Challenge/Criticality	Supplier	Solution

CHAPTER 6

Customer of Choice

How valuable would it be if you could gain preferential access to scarce resources? What would it mean for your business if suppliers brought their latest innovation and thinking to you first? What could be achieved if you only worked with the best people from your top suppliers and could secure preferential pricing?

You don't need to be the largest account to achieve this. You just need to position your business as a customer of choice. It is time to take an alternative approach to the buying and selling process and become the preferred sale point for your suppliers.

I'm not talking about a key account. This can be a large spend that covers fixed costs. Perhaps even a well-known brand. These accounts are not necessarily customers of choice as they may have low margins, be challenging to work with and may not appreciate a supplier's value-add.

Customer of choice status is harder to secure. There are relatively few for any one supplier. In some instances, it could be as few as five, often representing a single digit percentage of all customers sold to. This makes it a highly competitive position to hold.

WHY BOTHER

Would you allow your organisation to give up hard-earned, best practice information to your customers if they did not value you? I doubt it. Yet suppliers often find themselves in that position with some of their customers.

Does your business value key suppliers as highly as customers? Do you think you should? Let's consider that for a moment. Customers bring revenue, and key suppliers bring the necessary inputs. Without customers, you have no business and without suppliers, you may struggle to create and deliver what you sell. It doesn't matter if it's goods or services, your key suppliers are the lifeblood of your business. Sure you could change suppliers but if you keep down that path, you will never be a customer of choice. I would challenge you to re-assess the importance of your key suppliers to your business. Your actions should flow from there.

The organisation that buys seeks value for money. The organisation that sells seeks money for value. That's not to say that the buyer and seller have nothing in common. It means that if both recognise their part to play, then the goals can be seen as being in a constant state of positive tension. The ideal relationship occurs when that tension is in balance.

Not all tension is bad; think what would happen if there were no tension on your car's fan belt for instance. Positive tension stimulates innovation, whilst a lack of tension can stagnate an account on both sides of the table.

Ensure your supplier receives the right amount of money for the value they provide. Similarly, have your supplier ensure you receive optimum value for the money you are expending with them. This mutual consideration results in outcomes that can more easily meet the criteria for customer of choice and supplier of choice.

Procurement is the function that is responsible for this day-to-day supplier interaction and consequentially the quality of relationships that can develop. This requires the function to make a step change and become strategic in its behaviour. Encouragingly, this change is well within grasp.

WHAT'S IN IT FOR YOUR BUSINESS

1. **Preferential access to scarce resources.** Securing supply in a 'buyers' market is one thing; it's an entirely different matter when goods are either rare or extremely expensive. Consider what would happen to your operations if your key inputs were unavailable. Could you still supply your customers? Why would a supplier choose to supply their goods to your business over your competition? You have to present a compelling reason if you really want preferential access.

2. **Innovation potential.** What products could be created; what markets could be entered if your business was given the first right of refusal to the best thinking of your suppliers? The thing is, they are not just going to throw this knowledge around; there will be a careful assessment of all their current and potential clients to determine who would be best to work with.

   Stop and ask yourself, how many confidential innovations are your suppliers working on right now? Can you name them? If you don't know, if you're unable to list the critical projects, I can guarantee one thing—it's not that your suppliers aren't innovating, it is simply going to your competition.

3. **Preferential pricing.** If your business is the first point of call for all supplier developments, if the two companies are working collaboratively on a new project, then this is often accompanied

by favourable pricing. Clearly, the 'first to market' benefits that are associated with new technologies and early adoption carry development costs. Thankfully, paying for this development can be structured in many and varied ways that do not necessarily penalise your business for trying something new.

SELECTION CRITERIA

Positioning your business as a candidate for customer of choice status requires a deliberate and planned approach. There needs to be a demonstration over time that your business is the right company for a supplier to engage. So how is this done?

1. **The account (your business) needs to be sufficiently profitable:** This does not mean a supplier operates carte blanche with its prices. Pricing needs to have sufficient margins to make the account attractive and to allow for development although exorbitant margins are clearly not to be tolerated.

2. **Alignment of vision and direction:** The two companies need to have similarities in where they are headed. It makes working relations so much more compatible if you are heading for roughly the same goal. The path you take will no doubt be different but a common objective makes for easier discussion at the leadership level.

3. **Behaviours:** Statements and proclamations from procurement, business leadership, operations, etc., need to be backed up with action. The proof is always in the pudding so make sure that your business is easy to work with, engaged, receptive and inclusive. Don't forget the simple things like doing what you say, paying those invoices on time and leaving adversarial behaviour at the door.

4. **Potential:** Your business may not be the largest account with your supplier. From your supplier's perspective, if your requirements are profitable, aligned, and business is conducted with affirming behaviour, then the potential for a longer-term relationship is far higher. These accounts are highly favoured as they are the ones that will keep a supplier's doors open into the future.

WHAT'S IN IT FOR SUPPLIERS

Apart from the obvious benefits of profit and growth, a customer of choice often allows a supplier to make investments in capital equipment, systems, software, capability upgrades, formulation development and so on.

It is this activity that keeps their company, as it does yours, growing for the years ahead.

Suppliers are looking for and need customers of choice. So you have a choice; it can either be your business that works, collaborates and co-creates with a supplier, or it's your competition.

CASE STUDY: TELSTRA—STRATEGIC PARTNER PROGRAM

I spoke with Neil Rainey—General Manager of the Strategic Partner Program within Telstra. Neil, a long-standing executive and employee of the company, shared with me the ins and outs of this highly strategic function.

It's common knowledge that Telstra is a vast organisation. To help illustrate just how large, here are a few statistics to add weight.

Telstra spends AUD$10.6 billion a year on goods and services across more than 6,300 suppliers. There are almost 2,100 contracts actively managed and procurement touches everything from IT services to marketing, fleet and property. The procurement and supply chain payroll consists of 220 individuals.

It is staggering to learn that the top 100 suppliers account for 80 per cent of total annual spend. Even more astounding is that the top 10 suppliers make up 45 per cent of annual spend—that's AUD$4.7 billion spent each year with these suppliers. With a spend profile like that, it definitely warrants a unique supplier management model.

According to Neil, the Strategic Partner Program was created in 2012 as an answer to the question of how best to manage and use the most significant supply partners. In other words, how could Telstra harness supplier capabilities through a customer of choice arrangement?

The program is staffed by a team of five and is designed to harness the capability of Telstra's most significant supply partners so that the company can more effectively collaborate, communicate and innovate. This is achieved through a variety of means:

- Holding joint innovation laboratories and workshops
- Collectively going to market
- Developing joint marketing programs
- Arranging executive visits and information sharing.

What's telling here is that the above four criteria are in order of importance. This means that financial thresholds come later, and there is no mention of savings to be found.

Neil explained that to be a strategic partner with Telstra, there are certain criteria that need to be satisfied. The supply partner has to be able to help Telstra innovate, create great customer experiences, improve Telstra's competitive advantage and have an existing significant financial relationship.

The single largest driver of the program is the rapid speed of technology development. The whole program exists to extract maximum value from the supply partners and develop new growth opportunities.

What is interesting to note is that the program is independent of tactical procurement activities. Due to the size of the suppliers and the complexity of relationships, matters to do with price, contracts, compliance and risk are managed by tactical procurement. However, strategic relationships are managed separately by the Strategic Partner Program.

By developing and maintaining these strategic partnerships, the group can keep Telstra's executive informed through regular briefings, equipping these leaders with pertinent knowledge for their regular engagements with their counterparts from the supply program.

The size of Telstra's spend and the fast-paced change that the telecommunications industry experiences justifies this approach with suppliers. It helps this business stay one step ahead of the competition through partnerships that leverage the knowledge of other highly capable companies.

While this approach works for Telstra, it may not necessarily be suitable for mid-market companies. It is useful to understand how large, leading-edge corporations operate as this knowledge can help smaller businesses develop tailored fit-for-purpose programs.

COMMERCIAL TIE-BACK

Customer of choice status is hard to secure and challenging to retain. It will cost your business to be awarded this status. Yet, the benefits far outstrip the alternative, key-account ranking.

Let's consider a hypothetical scenario.

A critical supply partner brings novel technology to your company for first right of refusal. You discuss the various applications and how you could incorporate it into a confidential new product that your business is creating.

An exclusive contract is signed for a number of years. A patent and trademark are developed for the relevant geographic regions, and work begins tweaking the technology so that it fits with your product. In effect, the supplier's technology is now being built for your purposes.

The integration is completed, trials are performed, and a launch date is agreed upon. The new product hits the market providing something fresh and new. You have a monopoly on this for the next few years because of the licensing around the technology. This is more than enough time to command a premium sale price before your competition catches up.

While abridged in description, as it turns out this has more fact than fiction. It describes the situation that unfolded for a company I assisted, once they were seen as a customer of choice.

TOP TIPS

1. Identify those suppliers where your business would benefit from being positioned as a customer of choice.

2. Stop and consider what your suppliers think of your business. Do their actions affirm or contradict their words?

3. Consider whether your business views suppliers as important as customers. If so, why or why not?

PART 3

Innovation and Structure

CHAPTER 7

Innovation—Survive or Thrive

THE LAY OF THE LAND

If you are not innovating, you're going backwards.

Polaroid, Alta Vista, Kodak, Blockbuster, and Borders are all examples of companies that didn't innovate, and the consequence was their decline.

The marvellous thing about being a mid-market company is that such a business regularly retains the entrepreneurial leadership that took the business from infancy to its present capacity.

Beware the multi-national giant. Large organisations are beginning to change. They are grasping the need to evolve like start-ups and are using strategies to speed up development times and gain access to improved ways of working.

Consider the approach that GE and Barclays Bank take. General Electric has started using 'open innovation' whereby external engineers can take part in design competitions[1]. This extra mental mus-

---

[1] General Electric Open Innovation. Viewed 1 August 2016.
http://www.ge.com/about-us/openinnovation

cle is used to reduce development time and improve technical performance. Barclays Bank in London on the other hand has set up an Accelerator centre to partner with start-ups and help the bank capture, implement and promote technology change[2].

What are you doing to innovate? There is no time for mid-sized organisations to delay. As larger organisations begin to adopt innovative practices, competition will only increase. A big, fast, cashed-up, innovative and entrepreneurial company is something to be reckoned with.

INNOVATION AND BIG BUSINESS

Discovering new ways of working is the lifeblood of every business—or it should be.

Unilever estimates that around 70 per cent of their innovations are linked to their working relationships with strategic suppliers.[3] With a global turnover for 2015 of €53.3 billion, this puts perspective on just how significant this innovation activity would be.[4]

Similarly, Toyota aims to develop long-term supply relations that produce first-to-market innovation. Toyota was the first automotive company to launch the mass-produced hybrid vehicle—the Prius.

---

2 Barclays Bank Accelerator. Viewed 1 August 2016.
 http://www.barclaysaccelerator.com/#/

3 Trebilcock, B 2014, 'Unilever Partners to Win', *Supply Chain Management* Review, 24 September, viewed 13 May 2015,
 http://www.scmr.com/article/unilever_partners_to_win

4 Unilever 2016, *Highlights of Unilever's 2015 full year r*esults, 19 January,
 https://www.unilever.com/Images/q4-2015-highlights_tcm244-470011_en.pdf

Originally sold in 1997 only to the Japanese market, it was introduced globally from 2000 onwards.[5]

It is easy to forget that behind a launch of significant innovation comes vast amounts of research, development and expense. Toyota kicked off its G21 project in 1993 where it aimed to create a car for the 21st century. Initially focused on improved engine performance and fuel efficiency, the project shifted direction to focus on the development of a hybrid system. While the electric motor and inverter were manufactured by Toyota, the production of the nickel-metal hydride battery was tasked to Panasonic EV Energy Co.

The technology development was nothing short of astonishing. A fairly unknown and unproven science was taken to mass production in around two years from the official start of development.

Whatever you think of Toyota, or hybrid vehicles for that matter, the Prius has come into its own with fluctuating oil prices and increased awareness of environmental impacts.

It is that combination of innovation and the long-term view taken toward relationships with suppliers that has played such a crucial role in Toyota's success.

WE ALL LIKE PIZZA

There is the risk of a disconnect when citing the innovation activities of large companies such as Toyota and Unilever. Let's look at a more relatable example. There are plenty of smaller, yet highly innovative

---

5 Toyota 2012, *75 Years of Toyota: Prius development completed in approximately two years*, viewed 13 May 2015,
   http://www.toyota-global.com/company/history_of_toyota/75years/text/leaping_forward_as_a_global_corporation/chapter4/section8/item1_a.html

organisations that serve as great success stories, and Domino's is one of those.

John Harney, Dominos Group Chief Procurement Officer, spoke with me about how procurement operates in this business.

Before delving into the world of ham, cheese and tomato paste, it's worthwhile understanding a few details of the business as a whole.

Domino's Pizza started in 1983 as a single store in Springwood, Queensland, Australia. Now with more than 2,000 stores across seven markets (Australia, New Zealand, France, Belgium, Netherlands, Germany and Japan), this Australian business is the largest pizza chain in Australia in both network store numbers and sales. For the period FY14, the Australian-run, global network (there is another Domino's network in the US) had sales in excess of AUD$1.24 billion selling more than 90 million pizzas.

From the very beginning, the business was all about innovation and set the pace as the provider of 'firsts':

- It was the first pizza maker to offer home delivery.

- Domino's was the first and only pizza maker to list on the Australian Stock Exchange.

- In 2005, Domino's partnered with Telstra to launch the first Australian mobile phone ordering system.

- In 2006, the company launched the first online order tracker for customers.

- In 2012, it became the first pizza company in the world to offer ordering through Facebook.

The innovations continue. In 2014, the company trialled Google Glass in its head office store in the hunt for efficiencies. In 2014 the company appointed a Chief Digital Officer to work in partnership with the Chief Information Officer. In 2016, Domino's revealed its autonomous delivery prototype DRU, or Domino's Robotic Unit. A world-first initiative, the goal is to have food and beverage delivered via driverless vehicle.[6]

Where does procurement sit in all of this? As John explained, in the hunt for improvement in overall performance, Domino's draws the procurement function into the heart of all discussions.

In this business, procurement holds that often-coveted position of a seat on the board, due to its understanding of how to engage and contribute to business success. There is no siloed thinking here. Procurement spreads out across the entire company, contributing to all manner of conversations from IT to operations.

It is this knowledge and conviction that procurement can and does contribute to company success that sees the function embraced by its business partners.

When speaking with John, there was no shortage of passion and enthusiasm. One of the strong messages that came across was how the full procurement team believes in its ability to contribute to company growth and performance. Consequently, a positive, upbeat attitude resonates throughout the team.

John shared that while new ideas may come from any quarter of the business, all functions roll up their sleeves and draw together equally to deliver.

---

6 Dominos 2016, *Domino's Reveals Plans for World's First Commercial Autonomous Delivery Vehicle,* viewed 21 April 2016,
https://www.dominos.com.au/inside-dominos/media/march-2016-domino-s-reveals-plans-for-the-world-s-first-commercial-autonomous-delivery-vehicle

For example, in 2014 Domino's looked to motorised bicycles as an answer to generating yield improvements. Motorised bicycles are not your everyday procurement activity.

While the idea came from another team, procurement was engaged from the beginning in research, supply capability determination and to run the concept to ground. There was never any time for navel gazing and being precious about managing your own 'patch'. Each function was expected to contribute and contribute they did.

The project generated improvements in delivery times over cars and scooters due to the ability to avoid traffic and park right outside the customer's door—not the regular 100m or so down the road. The minimum age of drivers also fell to 16 years—no provisional licence requirements were needed here. This, in turn, reduced labour pay rates. It was also found that legislation requirements for bicycles globally are fairly consistent. This allowed for standardisation of design, with volumes able to be ordered en masse and through a single source.

As a second example, 2012 saw the introduction of flat-packed shop fronts. Traditionally purchased as individual components or through a contractor who fits out each property, Domino's looked to minimise expense by exploring the option of flat-packed kitchens. Although flat-pack as a concept is not new, it certainly was a leap for Domino's to move to this type of arrangement.

A high degree of collaboration took place to develop the specifications and locate appropriate suppliers. The difference in price allowed Domino's to use higher-end fixtures such as marble bench-tops, to increase the premium nature of the brand associated with the Domino's product.

So while the overall fit-out price was held flat (against a backdrop of rising labour and material costs), the quality was improved markedly to match the new positioning of the brand. Procurement was at the heart of making this possible.

John went on to share that even with all this innovation, Domino's is still looking at the second and third round of improvements. For instance, the next step in the shop fit-out process is to have all the wiring built in so it will just be a matter of assembling the shopfront and connecting electronics, further reducing expense and renovation timeframes.

Convention states that procurement in the food industry should only be involved in the sourcing of ingredients and packaging. The non-conventional nature of procurement activities within Domino's dispels that notion.

STRATEGIC PROCUREMENT AND INNOVATION

So procurement has a significant role to play when it comes to innovation. The function needs to understand that the company has a strategic direction and unpack new ways of working and thinking (often through suppliers or business partners) to accelerate this change.

If procurement's goal was all about cost reductions, then by that action, innovation would be stifled.

The role procurement can play is to produce faster and leaner processes with less waste, and not at the expense of your supply partner's margin.

You want your business to be profitable; the same is true for your suppliers. Let's put the shoe on the other foot. I highly doubt that you'd find it an attractive partnership arrangement if your customers were more interested in squeezing you for every last drop of savings, rather than letting you be profitable (reasonably, not exorbitantly). Profitability gives you funds to invest and experiment with new technology and ways of working that, in turn, can be passed on to your clients.

To not innovate means you are at best standing still or, more likely, going backwards. This is because your competition will be pushing towards faster, less expensive ways of working. They will be harnessing new technologies and applications to differentiate themselves and generate a competitive advantage.

HOW SHOULD SUPPLIERS BE MANAGED?

Innovation boils down to the exploration and sharing of knowledge. A sure-fire way of killing this creativity and lateral thinking is to have a procurement function that uses a 'big stick' as a management tool. Such a team will inevitably be driven by price, get bound up in the process and lack the foresight to see the potential from change.

There are a few straightforward and practical approaches that procurement should adopt to draw the most out of your supply partners:

1. **Business between equals:** Change your language. Refer to key suppliers as 'partners' not 'vendors'. This creates equality—a very important part of ensuring your suppliers know they are valued. Let's not confuse things. They are your supplier; you are their client. They have detailed knowledge of their goods and services, and you understand your operations inside out. These are different roles, yet complementary. Avoid the temptation to feel that because you are buying that makes you superior. Both sides of the transaction are equal; you pay an agreed fee, they supply the required goods and services. Because of the equality in the exchange, you would do well to treat your supply partners as equals too.

2. **Exchange of personnel:** Innovation takes off when both sides of the exchange clearly understand each other. In some instances, this can be enabled through a staff exchange or

embedding one of their team in your business. Remember—the end goal is improvement (whatever that may look like) so be prepared to try different approaches.

3. **Visit them:** Procurement regularly has suppliers visit them in their own offices. At worst there is a power play going on here; at best there is indifference on procurement's behalf in recognising the value of visiting suppliers. Whether they supply goods or services, the simple act of visiting your suppliers demonstrates your interest and commitment, increasing the prospect of success before work begins.

4. **Reward, don't just penalise:** Too many contracts aim to penalise for non-performance yet fail to recognise outstanding service and quality. Some companies believe that superior quality should be a given, and therefore, no recognition is warranted. While you are not going to continue to do business with a consistently underperforming supplier, it's important to remember that there is a human element at play here. We all value reward and recognition. An agreement that only focuses on penalties is one-sided and uninspiring. Innovation requires creativity and expansive thinking, something that can be stifled in these conditions. Secondly, the reward can take varying forms. Like innovation itself, think laterally about what this could look like for you.

COMMERCIAL TIE-BACK

We can't stop change, nor would you want to, but we can be left behind.

Innovation may come from within. However, a larger number of opportunities to grow and improve will more than likely come from your suppliers, customers, and collaborative partners.

Lucia Chierchia is the open innovation manager at Electrolux and is a part of their R&D team. In an interview with Procurement Leaders, Lucia said: "I see the research and development staff in suppliers as an extension of our own R&D (function)."[7]

That is a significant statement and not dissimilar to how a number of FMCG and electronics companies operate. By adopting this outward-looking approach, new ways of working are examined and explored.

Electrolux follows what it refers to as its 'Challenges Process' to access new innovation. This method is a five-step process:

1. The needs (or 'Challenges') of business are identified

2. Challenges are then launched to a network of current and prospective suppliers

3. A scouting exercise is performed

4. The merits of individual ideas and proposals are assessed

5. Preferred strategies are shared with the Electrolux Open Innovation Board, ahead of potential investment

As Electrolux demonstrates, there are companies out there that are great at innovating and working with suppliers. It's part of how they operate, and they have been doing it for years.

---

7 Rae, D 2015, 'Who should own Supplier-Enabled Innovation?', *Procurement Leaders*, 17 September, viewed 10 January 2016,
http://www.procurementleaders.com/blog/my-blog–david-rae/who-should-own-supplier-enabled-innovation-568086

If mid-market companies need motivation to innovate then look no further than large, cashed-up multinationals that have the resources to match their intent.

Ask yourself, how involved is procurement in the drive for innovation in your business?

As the conventional gatekeeper of suppliers and rapport, procurement is in the hot seat to help. Fill this team with the right-minded people and empower them for change and watch the opportunities unfold. Operational efficiencies, unit cost savings, faster processes, new products/services and the ability to surpass your competition—these are a few of the benefits that can come from drawing procurement into the innovation process.

TOP TIPS

1. Think about how your business presently invests in and researches innovation and the effectiveness of this approach.

2. Evaluate whether your supply base is effectively engaged when it comes to collaboration, innovation, and change.

3. Do you have an innovation funnel? If so, does this account for short, medium and long-term plans? Are your suppliers aware of this and how are they encouraged to participate?

CHAPTER 8

Beyond the 'Bottom Line'

WHAT DOES BUSINESS WANT?

We are living through one of the most exciting periods in history. The world's population is changing rapidly with a rising middle-class in much of Southeast Asia, India, China and North Africa. This population is earning more and looking for an increased standard of living.

Opportunity abounds to meet this growing demand, and many countries and organisations are responding to the need.

What are the strategic goals to which your company aspires? Greater market share through acquisition, growing international trade, increased organic growth (or 'wallet share'), healthier margins, perhaps improving capital funding and cash flow. It is a broad spread of considerations on the table.

Richard Savva, former Asia Pacific Director for ATPI and previously CEO of Voyager Travel, Australia's largest independent travel management company, spoke with me about prioritising the decisions that he must make as a leader.

Richard's remarks were straightforward. His top priority was to his staff. As a significant employer, he expressed the immediate need to take care of his team so that they could take care of their livelihood. He shared a genuine belief and responsibility to do all he can to give those who work for him every opportunity to succeed.

More than a corporate statement about staff being important assets, this was a deep-seated personal conviction arising from his time spent with the global travel business, Rosenbluth. This company took what some may see as the contrarian position of putting the employee first. Richard understands the need to take care of the team, as he says they, in turn, will take care of you.

Sustainable growth in turnover, infrastructure development, technology and winning new accounts were next in line for Richard. This was followed by satisfying shareholders and empowering executive management with the means of fulfilling the business' aims.

When I asked Richard about the challenges that he sees leadership facing, he cited the speed of change as the greatest problem to confront. "We're in a world where you can be out of date in 24 hours. But the expectation is you need to be in contact around the clock. The reality is that not every business has the capability to keep up with this demand."

It appears that Richard may not be alone with his beliefs about team and technology. In 2016, PwC released its 19th annual CEO survey.[1] Around 1,400 CEOs were interviewed globally from a range of regions and industries. Three of the key messages that emerged from this study were:

1. **Greater Expectations:** 52 per cent of CEOs claimed that profitability is encouraged by creating greater value for a wider pool of stakeholders.

---

1 PricewaterhouseCoopers 2016, *19th Annual CEO Survey*, viewed 21 April 2016, http://www.pwc.com.au/publications/ceo-survey-2016.html

2. **Transformation:** 90 per cent of CEOs looked at technology differently, changing how it can be used to deliver on stakeholder expectations.

3. **Measuring Success:** 76 per cent of CEOs agree that business success will be redefined by more than just financial profit.

Whether you agree with all, one or none of the above, the question remains, what are you hoping to achieve and how are ALL facets of your business (procurement included) contributing toward delivery? This is not just a question for the near-term; the current fiscal year, the present federal electoral cycle or the stable of work in-hand. It is a consideration that demands an answer now in order to fulfil tomorrow's medium to long-term strategies.

WINNER'S CURSE

How often do we find ourselves wanting a higher-quality product with enhanced service all for the same price? Everyone loves a great deal.

Rarely is something genuinely free. Providing a client with higher service levels or a more superior product can involve additional personnel, more time and an enhanced process. If the sale price does not move to compensate for this increased time and energy, then margin will be impacted.

Too often in business, we squeeze suppliers on price and expect the same or improved service, as well as quality. The relationship can then turn sour as expectations remain unmet, and service and quality suffers.

While we all want great value and savings from our suppliers, everything has a price.

This idea of moving away from a focus on savings is supported by the 'Winner's Curse'. As price decreases, ever diminishing levels of service and quality can be observed as margin pressure is felt and service can't be sustained.

A supplier might offer a reduced price in a tender and state that performance and quality are included. You need to question whether this is achievable. It's important to understand if the pricing offered is sustainable or if the company is trying to 'buy' your business, which could impact on service delivery.

If an account is 'bought', how will the supplier obtain cost recovery or make a profit? They will inevitably take a range of approaches that may include cutting corners, as well as creative and sometimes hostile interpretation of the scope. They may also attempt to secure additional funds from the client to allow for an increase in workload and quality.

One side of the Winner's Curse demonstrates that if you reduce price, it's fair to expect over time a reduction in service and quality. The other side of this argument is that if you maintain (or increase) the price, you have a means of ensuring that higher service and quality are delivered. The key is to develop a plan for generating greater commercial value from this higher service where the value delivered exceeds the differential in the price paid.

THE TRUE COST OF DOING BUSINESS

There is a hidden cost of doing business, something that appears benign, almost inconsequential and barely worth examination.

Sometimes skipped over by the mid-market is the cost and behaviours in the Purchase-to-Pay (P2P) cycle. How much it costs to raise a purchase order (PO), the cost of the current invoicing process, what a business may be doing to get around the process and the layers of approval— these are P2P considerations. Inefficiencies in this area can add significant expenses but are not explicit costs.

Martin Burgman is the Head of Procurement for Schenck Process Australia and has 17 years procurement experience working for a number of ASX 500 companies in mining, manufacturing, construction and service industries. He has worked on a number of business improvement programs and specialises in 'P2P Health', identifying the true cost of doing business as well as the gaps in systems, process or behaviour that lead to rework and inefficiency.

Martin says that for multinationals, there is a growing awareness of the need to address the P2P process. The increased level of complexity, which is often intrinsic to these organisations, presents a challenge that can be difficult to overcome.

As Martin describes, for the average company, 70 to 80 per cent of purchase orders have a spend value under AUD $1,000. Yet the total value of these purchase orders constitutes 5 to 20 per cent of total spend. The matter can be further compounded as some 50 per cent of all invoices often contain errors in the first pass, meaning that these invoices are moved to a 'parked and blocked' status. People tend to point the finger at Accounts Payable (AP) for delayed payments. If you dig a bit further, you will find the root cause is often in the P2P process; errors just manifest in AP.

What this says is that even for the most efficient system, considerable time can be spent processing a large quantity of invoices that constitute a small portion of spend. When you combine this with the need to rehandle around 50 per cent of your invoices, this adds considerable extra cost to address the errors.

It's not hard to see how these simple and often innocuous tasks can become very expensive. Yet for some businesses, it remains largely unseen.

As Martin says: "Systems will give you efficiency but behaviours provide effectiveness." It's this effectiveness that yields the larger commercial benefits.

Benefits from tackling the P2P challenge can be seen across two fronts.

1. If you can reduce the time and subsequent cost of raising a PO, then this price difference multiplied by the volume of POs can generate considerable benefits. The challenge is that it is hard to quantify the true cost of a PO, and it is difficult to see this benefit hit the bottom line of your business.

2. The more meaningful and quantifiable benefits and behaviours to monitor include: increasing levels of PO automation, reductions in invoices going to error, invoices arriving after the PO issue date (a good indication of governance) and increasing the speed from cheque to requisition. The effect of this can result in faster turnaround times, the ability to reduce payroll costs and/or the freeing up of team members to take on other projects.

Companies can adopt one of two methods to respond to this situation—outsource the process or buy technology. While both will deliver improvements, outsourcing can move an existing problem to someone else. The risk—if it is not resolved, it's just further out of reach.

Martin makes it clear that technology alone will not fix a problem—it's the underlying process and human behaviours that need to be resolved.

The challenge with any P2P process arises when people get involved, or as Martin puts it: "Whenever you put the human between the technology there is the potential for error."

Procurement can establish the best possible supplier arrangements and pricing and yet these benefits can be largely eroded in the back-end. In other words, the benefit gained through effective negotiations and contacts can be neutralised by the cost of the P2P process. This is one of the reasons why it can be hard to see savings flow through to the bottom line.

I would be the last to advocate establishing a procurement function that is only concerned with control, process, risk, and monitoring. However, the piece of the P2P pie missing in mid-tier business is the presence of fit-for-purpose monitoring, reporting, and compliance. For a P2P program to succeed, it will need purchasing guidelines and governance. You will need to recognise and remove prior poor behaviours and establish a set of procedures, so the whole business operates from the same playbook.

So what options exist to perform a P2P assessment and improvement program? There are three choices:

1. **Do it yourself:** Do you have sufficient budget to add dedicated resource(s)? For any program to be successful, there needs to be a willingness to look in all the dark corners and appreciation that there is room for improvement.

2. **Buy-in labour:** Gain access to external resources (outsource or consultant). This is typically less expensive overall but without guidelines to sustain performance, the problems may not be completely resolved.

3. **Technology:** Systems are great but they often do not entirely solve the problem. You will still need to address past behaviours. While full-service systems are available, fee-for-service and subscription-based models are also emerging.

COMMERCIAL TIE-BACK

It's fair to say that for many companies, savings will always be a hot agenda item. With that in mind, there is more than one way to tackle this challenge.

Improving your company's back-end processes may not be glamorous but it can offer rich rewards.

Let's run a hypothetical scenario to map out potential benefits.

Purchase to Pay Scenario

Consideration	Value
Company turnover	$400,000,000
Total spend with suppliers	$200,000,000
Total number of POs raised annually	30,000
Number of POs with values <$1,000 (~70%)	22,000
Cost of a PO/Invoice (manual)	$15
Cost of a PO/Invoice (automated)	$5
Number of invoices parked and blocked (50% of all POs)	15,000
Cost of manual rework (15,000 × $15)	$225,000

Solution	Potential Savings
1. Automate PO generation process (30,000 × ($15–$5)	$300,000
2. Remove the need for rework	$225,000
Total Potential Savings	$525,000

The above P2P scenario is a high-level illustrative example of what funds could be saved by automating low-value transactions and minimising the rework of POs or invoices. Since every business is different, naturally the potential benefits will vary too.

TOP TIPS

1. Consider your company's objectives for the near, mid and long term. Identify how procurement could be directed to have a blend of short-term savings contributions and longer-term growth objectives.

2. In your company, does procurement aim to continually reduce supplier spend while still expecting increased service and performance? Consider how this could be changed to encourage higher supplier engagement.

3. Calculate what your P2P process is costing your business. Identify what can be done to improve and reduce this back-end expense.

CHAPTER 9

Aligned for Results

The late Steve Jobs, and former CEO of Apple, was famously quoted as saying: "It's in Apple's DNA that technology alone is not enough — that it's technology married with liberal arts…that yields us the result that makes our hearts sing."[1] What could that mean?

Every product that Apple creates needs to exemplify cutting-edge technology and the best possible experience for the consumer. Whatever your opinion is of Apple or Jobs for that matter, when we see the range of products that Apple has created we see how these principles have been implemented. The iPod, iPhone, iPad, and iTunes itself have all been firsts in commercialising new technology and yet also great experiences for the consumer.

Leading edge technology and design are what defines Apple. Every part of the organisation needs to (and still does) pull together to meet and live out this corporate goal and vision.

What is the vision for your company?

---

1 Elmer-DeWitt, Philip 2011, 'Steve Jobs' post-PC credo', *Fortune*, 4 March, viewed 28 June 2015, http://fortune.com/2011/03/04/steve-jobs-post-pc-credo/

LINES OF REPORTING

There are some functions in a business where it's clear where they should sit. A factory sits under operations, management accounting reports to finance and talent management resides within HR. When it comes to procurement, where should it sit within your organisational structure? It is not always so clear.

This is not semantics. Each department has a set of goals, often unique to their discipline. Hopefully, the collective goals across a business complement the overall company strategy that may include growth, profit, increased market share and so on.

Sometimes, the goals of one team do not always support those of another. For example, marketing may be incentivised to release a swag of new products that require a lot of operational trials. However, operations may have a target to run plant and equipment uninterrupted at the highest possible levels of capacity and efficiency. Procurement may then be told to save money wherever they can and look to rationalising marketing, advertising, and promotional activities and push operations to achieve even greater efficiency gains.

In what ways do the targets of your divisions clash?

Consider where procurement sits within your organisation. Some believe it should sit under finance while other schools of thought believe operations are a better custodian of the function. Wherever the procurement function is housed, its targets will be influenced by those to which it answers.

As every business is different, there is no clear-cut answer on what structure is best. Consider whether you want the function to be strategic in nature, flexible in approach, better aligned with business and bring rounded commercial insights. If this is how you want your procurement function to grow then ask yourself, will the current structure allow for this or is change needed?

WINNING HEARTS

Procurement's measuring stick for many companies has been, and will continue to be, savings.

For some businesses, savings appear lower down on the list of priorities as the true value of the procurement function lies in more than cost reductions.

Bruce Beeren was a Non-Executive Director of Origin Energy from 2005–2014. Prior to this role, he was the company's Finance Director from 2000–2005, reporting to the CEO Grant King. It was as Finance Director that Bruce had procurement and the CFO independently reporting directly to him.

Origin Energy, through its LNG project, has grown to become a significant organisation. Yet, even back in 2005, Bruce's last year as Finance Director, the company was still of substantial size with an AUD $4.9 billion turnover.[2]

Although he had never worked in the procurement profession, Bruce demonstrated insightfulness into how to draw out the best performance.

When we spoke, Bruce shared that he believes procurement's main aim should be to "win the hearts and minds of the business, then deliver the savings. To get the savings, you need people to accept procurement. To get them accepting, you need to sell it". This simple remark is powerful. For Bruce, what comes first is people, rapport and trust as well as a genuine understanding of the needs of others. What naturally follows is that procurement goes on to deliver commercial gains.

---

2 Origin Energy 2005, *Opportunities through diversity—Annual Report 2005*, viewed 1 May 2016, https://www.originenergy.com.au/content/dam/origin/about/investors-media/docs/annual-report-2005.pdf

To try and tackle the objective from the other direction—savings first then win over the business—is bound to be a harder fought battle with potentially fewer returns.

What Bruce also emphasised was that a passive, subservient, under-resourced function with limited skills would never win the respect of peers and leadership. Procurement needs to fight for influence and go on to demonstrate ability. Any other course risks a loss of significance and influence.

Peter Turner became the Head of Procurement at Origin Energy, reporting directly to Bruce, during that time. I spoke with Peter, and he recalled one of his first planning meetings. He had come prepared for Bruce to discuss budgets, efficiencies and savings targets. What followed was not expected. Bruce remarked, "If I judge you on savings alone, one of two things will happen. Eventually, we will end up paying nothing for everything or else you will fail."

This is a surprising statement to originate from a Finance Director.

It wasn't just Peter who Bruce surprised—he caught my attention when he shared his opinion that the best model for procurement is when it does not report to the CFO.

Bruce understood, instinctively, that year-on-year expense reductions produce diminishing returns and if left for long enough become nigh on impossible to deliver. He also understood that when procurement reports to a CFO, inevitably savings will become a primary deliverable. This can put procurement on a collision course with the business where little consideration may be given to 'winning hearts and minds.'

Under Bruce's leadership at Origin, savings were not the only target or measurement for success. There was a need to show commercial value and ongoing improvement. However, it was how this value was delivered which was key for success for Bruce.

Reducing the cost base in business should always be a target but not the only target. It's a bit like you breathe to live not live to breathe.

Procurement's results would be measured on 'value' delivered to the business. Value can be interpreted in many ways. In Origin at this time, value was satisfaction levels held by executive general management that procurement activities were contributing to the growth and progression of each business unit.

The procurement function moved from being a corporate team, separated from operations and fixated on savings, to one with the sole purpose to align, embed and understand each division and help in the delivery of functional and company targets.

COMMUNICATING FOR RESULTS

Oliver Wendell Holmes Sr, a well-known American physician, poet, professor, lecturer and author in the 1800s, said: "Speak clearly, if you speak at all; carve every word before you let it fall."

This could not be more relevant than when communicating to a corporate audience.

There was a period in my career where I worked in heavy industry. My employer was a vertically integrated organisation that had mining operations at one end of the supply chain, steel manufacturing facilities in the middle and industrial steel sales at the other. The diverse spread of operations meant that divisions were quite different (or so they liked to think) and an overarching group procurement team needed to be careful how strategies were communicated.

As there was no mandate to make sweeping change, stakeholders needed to be engaged at all levels and an awareness of particular 'sensitivities' was paramount. The procurement team spent considerable effort crafting communication plans, gathering lists of words and phrases that could, and importantly should not be used when communicating change.

Looking back, it sounds excessive. At the time, the practical reality was that strategies could meet an abrupt end if a division was not carefully managed.

The message is simple enough.

Procurement's communication with its internal stakeholders should never be haphazard or unplanned. Instead, a structured and deliberate plan should be in place to ensure the best message is shared from the outset.

Have the team try these approaches to improve the effectiveness of communication:

1. Whenever possible, communication with internal stakeholders is best delivered face-to-face. Procurement needs to be a visible force that is actively seeking time with its internal business partners. It's this time that helps build confidence and trust for the future.

2. Canvas opinions broadly. A solution stands or falls on the strength of an argument. Procurement engaging with a wider audience produces 'rounded' solutions, preventing outcomes being built on the narrow opinions of a few.

3. Gauge the 'climate' of the audience to determine the best timing for an information release.

4. Announcements should always be a reminder for stakeholders, never breaking news.

5. Repackage the message for each audience. Recycling the same message for different audiences is not only lazy but unwise.

Let's assume procurement has developed a new strategy. How this is shared will differ from function to function:

- Finance—should have the commercial benefits emphasised.

- Operations—the favourable impacts on plant efficiency may be communicated.

- Marketing—how the strategy will assist growth or increase market share needs to be demonstrated.

Communication should be delivered with aplomb. It is a skill that requires polish, tact, and a strategic plan. An ill-thought-through approach can be detrimental. A carefully timed and worded sharing of information can gather individuals to unite for a common goal.

STAKEHOLDERS AND THEIR RESULTS

'Meet early, often, face-to-face and at their place.' This is a simple mantra that I have applied throughout my career, first as an employee and now as the Director of Synthesis Group.

It has a neutralising effect, resolving challenges before they take hold. It removes the power play of procurement's territorial advantage. It builds trust from the outset and allows for clear and unimpeded communication.

Peter Drucker, the Austrian-born American management consultant, educator and author said: "The most important thing in communication is hearing what isn't said."

While much of what we do as professionals is visible and on display to others, there is often an undercurrent in business. This undercurrent may sometimes be positive and at other times negative. It's the unspoken opinion, the closed-door discussion, the secret fear and the masked ambition that will scupper a carefully thought out but ill-communicated plan.

This approach of meeting early, often, in person and not on your ground removes the elephant from the room. It allows for more open, honest and transparent rapport and communication.

Often, it is the simple things, the subtle differences that procurement needs to become more skilled at to increase effectiveness in business.

Consider these five straightforward steps that will serve as indicators of procurement's success. How well does your procurement team apply them?

1. **Wants vs. Needs:** What a stakeholder wants is not always what they need. Procurement needs the insight and courage to carefully convey the alternative solution or additional element to a project. People are often open to change. Time should be taken to listen to their needs and what they value; only then present suggestions and improvements. The clincher—solutions must display evidence that procurement has indeed listened.

2. **Drivers:** What is the undercurrent of a function or an individual? What motivates them? What are their challenges and fears, hopes and aspirations? Procurement should not be afraid to show a human side too. We should strive to be individuals who can identify with others. If we can be relatable and aware of the business environment, it encourages others to open up areas that may have previously been inaccessible and convert opponents to advocates.

3. **Professional Persistence.** A willingness to remain connected and engaged takes tenacity, even when results don't come as quickly as planned. Demonstrating a desire to help achieve oth-

ers' targets is a professional attribute in short supply. A willingness to go the extra mile with stakeholders will be returned in kind, well beyond what it cost you initially.

4. **The Roving Professional.** Nothing is more powerful than being seen onsite, in the trenches, speaking with the team and working out of their 'territory'. In-business placement (even if only temporary) increases the likelihood of problem identification and resolution, trust, workable solutions and program success. This shows procurement cares, rather than the alternative of agitating for change from the safety of head office.

5. **A Responsibility to Educate.** The sharing of information and the education of others is a responsibility. It is not about being right or having authority over others; it's an opportunity to tactfully challenge prevailing process and provide options and better strategy.

In business, there will always be politics and strategies—in effect corporate games. Most of these tactics you would hope would be for the greater good, yet some of these approaches only serve the immediate interest of the individual.

All professionals, procurement included, need to rise above self-interest and consider the needs of others and the company at large. When this is performed with commercial precision, thorough knowledge of the subject matter and a focus on what is ahead tomorrow rather than what's in our hands today—it's this approach that rapidly and constructively changes business.

COMMERCIAL TIE-BACK

There are times when organisations have areas of un-addressable spend or projects for which procurement is not given access. They remain off limits and are managed only by those with proven capability and performance.

The exclusion of procurement could be due to the technical nature of the area, perhaps the criticality to business operations or maybe because it has just done a lousy job in the past.

Without question, new opportunities are more likely to arise with procurement's inclusion. It's common for fresh eyes to reveal different ways of working and more robust solutions.

For instance, when I was engaged to help one of Australia's larger agribusiness companies, in an assessment of their operations, more than 30 areas for review and improvement were uncovered. Another example was providing assistance to a large outsourced medical services company. In a little more than two hours, eight significant areas for improvement were identified.

Yet, it all hinges on trust. Procurement must build trust with its stakeholders, understand their business and contribute toward the delivery of their targets.

TOP TIPS

1. List the areas of your business (spend or categories) that are currently off limits for procurement. Consider whether their reintroduction could add value and how.

2. For procurement to deliver its own and broader company targets, examine how the current reporting structure could change.

3. Review the communication methods that procurement currently uses. Consider how these can be improved for more effective results delivery.

PART 4

The Procurement Toolbox

CHAPTER 10

Prepare for the Unexpected

I remember in the early days of my career arriving at work to the news that, overnight, the manufacturing facility of an offshore packaging supplier had been destroyed by fire.

The impact would be significant. There was a long lead-time to bring product in from overseas. We would need to find a new supplier, develop tooling, validate, perform trials and enter production in a tight timeframe to keep our product flowing to the customer.

I began to get an inkling of the considerable workload and manic operations that lay ahead. Through the mental fog, I remember my manager appearing calm. What was shared next has profoundly influenced how I have worked since. "It's nothing to worry about; we've already implemented the disaster recovery plan."

A concept that was new to me at the time, this disaster recovery plan proved to be one of the most significant 'insurance' policies a company could hope to have.

Manufacturing was moved, within two weeks, to an alternative location where the tooling, capacity, and materials had all been pre-validated. Production commenced and product was shipped without delay.

Despite the highly disruptive nature of the incident, the manufacturing of product continued and not a ripple was felt by our customers.

Remarkable by all accounts. That is until it's understood just how well-prepared and planned the business was to deal with such an event. It wasn't remarkable at all, just a telling example of thorough and proactive strategic procurement in practice.

PROGRAM PURPOSE

Disaster recovery and contingency planning can be wrapped up neatly under Crisis Management Planning ('Plan').

While the nature of the threats can vary, the intent is one and the same—develop a measured and even-handed response—so that no matter if you sell goods or services, when faced with disruption you can quickly return to standard operations.

The heat of a crisis is not the time or the place to develop a disaster response. A successful solution requires preparation and pre-validation. Hopefully, the Plan will never have to be used. Thankfully, it is in place should you ever need to draw upon it.

This is a dynamic strategy, and so it requires regular appraisal to ensure its currency. Implementation should be as simple as flicking a 'switch', but this is only made possible with detailed planning and established accountabilities.

THREATS

I want to draw a distinction here. The risks in business are far broader than the threats being addressed in a crisis management plan.

As Aon point out in their *2014 Australasian Risk Survey*, risk concerns in business can be everything from regulatory and legislative change, local and global economic conditions, increasing competition, risks to brand and human resources.[1]

These areas of risk go well beyond the mechanics of doing business and extend into the arena of insurable and uninsurable social, political and economic factors, an area for the insurance companies. This chapter will help you to identify and manage threats to business operations.

What constitutes a threat is anything that has the potential to significantly disrupt the normal course of business.

Let's be clear, while your business may not sell tangible goods, a company that provides services, software and cloud-based technologies is just as exposed. You may not have a factory that could be destroyed, yet there will be intangible assets that could be compromised, corrupted or copied.

The Global Economic Crime Survey 2016 released by PwC indicates that business is not keeping pace with cyber threats.[2] The survey indicates that Cybercrime is now the 2nd most reported economic crime and affects 32% of organisations. Of particularly concern is that only 37% of organisations have a response plan, consequentially, most companies remain ill-prepared.

Threats will vary between industries and can in some instances be very specific. Some of the more common threats that organisations may face include:

---

1   Aon 2014, *Aon's 2014 Australasian Risk Survey*, viewed 20 April 2015
    http://www.aon.com.au/australia/thought-leadership/risk-survey.jsp

2   PricewaterhouseCoopers 2016, *Global Economic Crime Survey 2016*, viewed 28 April 2016
    http://www.pwc.com/crimesurvey

- Departure of key personnel
- Heavy dependence upon one or a handful of critical goods, services or clients
- Inadequate contractual instruments
- Cyber or physical attack
- Product recalls and contaminations
- Natural disaster or Acts of God
- Destruction or failure of assets
- Biological agents

Generating a list of possibly threats is one thing, it's an entirely different matter when we recall actual events. The 2014 AirAsia crash, the 2010 BP Deepwater Horizon drilling rig accident and oil spill, and 2005's Hurricane Katrina in the US all serve as reminders of what can happen when things go terribly wrong. Sometimes we have control and in other circumstance we are at the mercy of the elements.

While we strive to prevent these events, protect life and limit damage, it's up to us to make sure business is prepared to weather, recover and assist others in a crisis.

WHAT WILL IT COST?

In 2013, the World Economic Forum produced a report in collaboration with Accenture, *Building Resilience in Supply Chains.*[3] The report documented that significant supply chain disruptions have the effect of reducing the share price of affected companies on average by seven per cent.

This study was based on an analysis of 62 supply chain disruptions that were publicly announced during 2005-2011. These announcements appeared in a range of financial journals and publications and were about publicly traded companies that experienced production complications, shortage of parts and supply chain issues due to natural disasters.

The report noted, amongst other findings:

1. The longer it took to resolve a disruption, the more negative its impact.

2. 80% of companies worldwide see better protection of supply chains as a priority.

3. Increased volatility is the new normal for interconnected supply chains.

So how would a crisis impact your business? What would be the resulting financial consequence from a disruption to operations and / or sales? I'd suggest the following would be high on the list.

- Substantial costs for recovery and repair

---

3 World Economic Forum 2013, *Building Resilience in Supply Chains—An Initiative of the Risk Response Network in collaboration with Accenture*, Industry Agenda, http://www3.weforum.org/docs/WEF_RRN_MO_BuildingResilienceSupplyChains_Report_2013.pdf

- Immediate loss of sales revenue

- Impacts upon future earning potential

- Competitors presented with an opportunity to strengthen market position

To emphasise the impact, let's consider costs from just one perspective—IT.

IBM and Ponemon Institute conducted a study in 2013 of more than 2,300 business and IT security professionals to calculate the cost of IT security failures.[4]

In this study, they asked respondents to estimate the duration, cost and likelihood for minor, moderate and substantial disruptions.

It was reported that minor events would last on average almost 20 mins, had an average cost of USD $53,000 per min and had a 69% likelihood of occurring in a two-year period. By contrast, the average impact of a major event was 442 mins in length, $32,000 per min in cost and 23% likelihood of occurring.

Through a multiplication of the average event length by the cost per min, the total cost for each event type can be determined. IBM estimated that a minor event would cost a business on average $1mil USD, a moderate event $4.3mil and a substantial disruption would cost a company on average $14.3 mil for an IT security event.

The message is simple enough. Disruptive events not only affect the operations of business but future earning potential and shareholder returns. When these costs are combined, it can build to a surprisingly large figure. Could your business afford such an event?

---

4 IBM November 2013. *Understanding the economics of IT risk and reputation: Making the business case for business continuity and IT security*, Viewed 10 August 2016.
    http://www-935.ibm.com/services/us/gbs/bus/html/risk_study/infographic-01.html

THE CHALLENGES FACED

Darren Bryan is an insurance specialist and has been in the risk industry for more than 25 years. He has worked in Australian and London markets for international insurance broking and risk advisory firms, helping both private and public sector clients.

Darren shared the three main challenges that he sees time and again with business when trying to develop a Plan and manage risk.

1. **Enabling company objectives.**

    Crisis Management Plans that are overly complex require considerable management, are slow to execute and will end as an encumbrance rather than an enabler. Alternatively, Plans can be too 'lite' in content and actionable process, doing little to protect the interests of the company.

    The strategic goals of your company need to be clearly identified in the Plan and measures need to be put in place to ensure they can be achieved, come what may.

    The cookie-cutter approach will rarely be sufficient. If you go to great lengths to differentiate your business from your competitors, how could a plan that is generic in structure possibly serve to protect your unique interests?

2. **Securing senior management buy-in.**

    Crisis management plans hinge upon the complete and unwavering support, contribution and accountability of senior management. A Plan is destined for failure if it only has senior management's tacit endorsement or was developed without their knowledge or input.

    When trouble strikes, the leadership in business pull out all stops to resolve the issue. If leadership is unaware, or not accountable and involved in the building and management of these Plans, the process is likely to be sidestepped. When your business needs a steady hand and a structured response, it finds itself without a clear plan and with compromised accountability.

3. **Documentation of risk is not management of risk.**

Just because a Plan has been developed doesn't mean it will work. The true genius of contingency planning is in its continual assessment, modification and improvement, not in its generation.

For example, your Plan may identify an alternative supplier. You have validated their process, systems, capability, and capacity. You enter into an understanding that they will be engaged in the event of a crisis. The Plan is signed and filed, and no further management is performed.

One month later, your contingent supplier wins a huge piece of work for a multi-year term and in their excitement, they neglect to tell you that they no longer have the capacity for your volumes. Right then your Plan is worth about as much as the paper it's printed on – and the terrifying thing is, you don't even know it!

PREPARING THE PLAN

Once the decision has been made to create a Plan, how should you start? Considerable detail can be documented—how much will be dependent upon your company's tolerance for risk. I have outlined a handful of areas for consideration. This is far from an exhaustive list but it will help you commence the process.

1. When developing a crisis management plan, make sure it considers risk across the breadth of your business including (but not limited to): facilities and tangible assets, people, intellectual property, computing technology, suppliers, contracts, and data.

2. Rank the risk. It's logical for risk to be initially measured in terms of severity. For instance, the risk to inventory levels is not as critical as the risk to life. The other axis that should be considered is criticality. What will cause your business discomfort and what will force the doors to close?

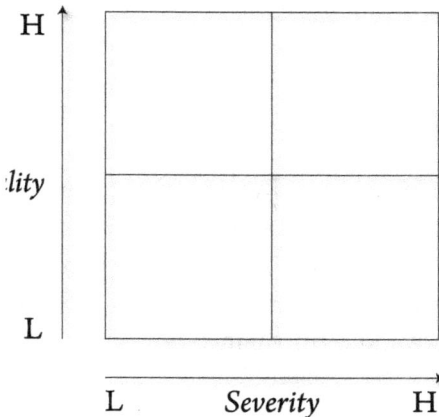

Ranking the Risk

3. Having been ranked by severity and criticality, each risk should then be assessed along a 'Likelihood' scale. The far left will feature those risks that are unlikely to occur, with a growing probability of an event taking place the further right the risk is placed.

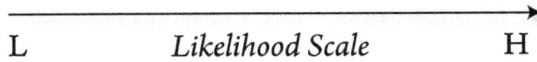

L   *Likelihood Scale*   H

The Scale of Likelihood

4. As with the chain of command in armed services, junior officers need to learn the role of their superiors. The same is true in business—make sure there is contingency built into the differing levels of responsibility.

5. Test it. Paper-based plans that don't go through live drills can be fraught with problems in the single instance where you need everything to just work.

FRENCH FRY SHORTAGE

In late 2014, a simmering dispute in the US between the Pacific Maritime Association and the International Longshore and Warehouse Union came to a head.[5] Contract negotiations broke down and consequentially, the Union was accused of slowing operations, maritime workers in some ports walked off their jobs.

5 Khouri, A 2014, 'West Coast port slowdown raises fears of dockworker strike or lockout', *Los Angeles Times*, 10 November, viewed 20 April 2015
http://www.latimes.com/business/la-fi-port-negotiations-20141111-story.html

The result—significant shipping congestion. Consequentially, many companies experiencing temporary shortfalls in stock.

McDonald's Japan was one organisation impacted by this dispute. The Japanese arm of McDonald's was unable to secure its regular quota of potatoes from the US. Consequently, a shortfall in the famous 'French Fry' was experienced and rationing measures were introduced.[6]

Granted this is a first world issue, who would have imagined that the globally recognised 'French Fry' would be in limited supply? The equally famous catch-cry, "Would you like fries with that" would no doubt have been rationed too.

Left scrambling to find alternative supplies, emergency stocks had to be air freighted and alternate sea channels used, yet still these efforts were not enough to overcome the shortfall.[7] It is reasonable to assume that these emergency measures would have been expensive and not sustainable for the long term.

Could McDonald's have prevented this?

It's expected that a company the size of McDonalds would have a crisis management plan in place. Whilst the maritime issues would be beyond their control, what about other factors? What about alternative pre-validated supply options (domestic and abroad), secondary freight arrangements and ongoing validity of supply capacity. Perhaps these angles had been considered and implemented. Only McDonalds would be able to shed light on what was done and how effective these measures were.

---

6 'Japanese McDonald's rations french fries, serves only small portions amid shortage' 2014, *ABC Online*, 17 December, viewed 15 April 2015,
http://www.abc.net.au/news/2014-12-16/mcdonalds-japan-rations-chips-amid-shortage/5971842

7 Fifield, A 2014, 'McDonald's is running out of French fries in Japan', *The Washington Post*, 16 December, viewed 15 April 2015,
https://www.washingtonpost.com/news/worldviews/wp/2014/12/16/you-want-fries-with-that-in-japan-you-can-only-get-a-small-order-at-mcdonalds/

From the safety of the armchair, it's all too easy to put forward solutions that may alleviate or prevent a crisis. The business that has weathered the storm is the only one that can say with certainty if they were prepared and did all they could.

How ready is your company for the unexpected?

TRAPS TO AVOID

1. **Delayed implementation.** Plan development is one of those tasks that when business is humming can be seen as important but non-urgent. I cannot stress this enough, now is the time to build the Plan. Trying to develop a successful response during a disaster event is like jumping off a cliff and hoping to build a plane on the way down.

2. **Assumptions.** It is easy to take answers at face value. It is not that your team or suppliers are being deliberately untruthful, it's that we may believe what others tell us without critically assessing the facts. When developing a crisis management plan, there can be no room for waffle or 'leaky' argument.

3. **Solutions fall short.** Let's say your digital information is hosted by an off-site server so now the local risk has been largely eliminated. Sounds good, but it could be better. A process whereby the third party server is tested for random file retrieval, maybe declaring a trial disaster scenario or perhaps creating a mirroring server arrangement would all go a long way in ensuring the service delivers on the intended purpose.

4. **Test for effectiveness.** Say your business is in the services industry. You have a number of integral and high-profile employees—one leaves. What strategies are in place to prevent clients

and other team members following the departing employee? This happens with partners in large law firms regularly. What is the plan to ensure the satisfaction of clients and the team?

5. **Who's accountable?** Crisis management plans need an owner internally and with the supplier. Keep the 'cooks' to a minimum but ensure those who have been tasked with management understand the Plan intimately and keep the business abreast of change.

COMMERCIAL TIE-BACK

Without question, the commercial opportunities from a crisis management plan are continuity of supply, maintaining the ability to operate and preventing or reducing supply disruptions to your customers.

In spite of this, not all companies have a Plan. Partial or complete disruption of supply to your clients not only has the immediate negative financial impact on sales, but it also can have the consequential impact of damaging consumer/client confidence, tarnishing your brand and surrendering market share to competition.

You don't leave the growth of your business to chance, why allow unnecessary risk to compromise your operations? I'd encourage you to take the time to plan and prepare.

To get a gauge for the type of commercial impact that could be experienced under a crisis, a non-exhaustive list of potential direct and indirect costs have been outlined below. What costs could impact your company?

Commercial Consequences of a Crisis

Direct Costs	Indirect Costs
1. Damaged / compromised goods and services: • Cost of writing off damaged stock and services • Replacement costs for stock and services • Premium unit pricing as goods and services are purchased in smaller multiples and short lead times	1. Lost Revenue: • Product and service unavailability creates a decline in consumer confidence • Product delisting and order cancellations from customers may occur.
2. Labour: • Specialised labour costs for restoration services • Un-forecast labour requirements from staff to return operations to a state of normality	2. Market Share: • Decline in market share due to unavailability • Strengthening of competitor's product appeal since your own product is unavailable.
3. Logistics: • Premium freight and handling costs for urgent delivery of plant and equipment	3. Contractual Penalties: • An inability to supply the stated goods / services to a client can initiate contract penalty clauses
4. Facilities: • Repair / rebuild damaged facilities	4. Reputation and brand: • Damage to brand and credibility
5. Forensics: • Discovery and audit costs to identify the cause of failure and prevention of reoccurrence	5. Compliance: • Restorative expenses, compensation and fines arising from the failure

TOP TIPS

1. Identify the disaster events that could significantly disrupt or cripple your organisation.

2. Evaluate the likelihood of these events taking place and how you may be able to anticipate them.

3. For the top three events, identify what financial impact would result if they were to occur.

CHAPTER 11

Mergers and Acquisitions

Your board has decided to make an acquisition. It could be a competitor or maybe a supplier to expand the depth of offering. You may be a veteran at this game or maybe this is the first time. No matter—you will be surrounded by your team, the team of the business you are acquiring, lawyers, accountants, consultants, bankers...and the list continues.

It's always good advice to stick to your knitting and let others share their knowledge in their areas of expertise. So with that in mind, I'm only going to discuss where and how procurement can contribute throughout the merger and acquisition (M&A) process.

This chapter is aimed at the business owner and executive team that acquires for strategic reasons that might include growth and profit, increased market share, new technology, new clients and so on. It focuses on trade-related acquisitions or sales since procurement has the potential to provide the greatest level of support and impact under these circumstances, in contrast to an acquisition conducted by a financial investor.

VERTICAL OR HORIZONTAL

Irrespective of the reason to buy, trade related acquisitions fall into one of two planes—vertical or horizontal acquisitions.

Vertical acquisitions are when a purchase is made up or down the supply chain; that is, a supplier or customer is acquired.

A supplier may be purchased to resolve a persistent shortage in supply. Perhaps it's due to your dependence on a particularly key material, or maybe your competitors also buy that material, and you wish to control supply, regulate their access and ensure your growth potential.

Alternatively, you may choose to purchase a customer. Since there already exists a link between the organisations, there is scope for an acquisition to:

- Provide access to a new market and customers.

- Allow the sale of a broader range of established product lines.

- Provide further established distribution channels for the buyer's product.

Horizontal acquisitions are the other direction and involve the purchase of a competitor. Typically, horizontal acquisitions are performed because it is believed that opportunities exist to:

- Operate the competitor more efficiently.

- Take advantage of larger economies of scale.

- Limit the competition within the industry in which you operate.

The 2009 acquisition of Bartter Enterprises by Baiada Poultry illustrates this point.[1] The acquisition of its competitor literally doubled Baiada's size, making it the largest provider of chicken meat to the Australian market, opening up a wider sales network that had been previously difficult to access.

PROCUREMENT AND ACQUISITIONS

The inconvenient nature of acquisitions is you may not know when one is going to take place. While a certain proportion of sales are initiated by the seller, there are others that are only announced when someone arrives at the door with an offer to buy your business.

As a member of the executive, you are expected to know what is required and how to progress through a transaction (irrespective if it goes ahead or not).

It's one thing to lean on the lawyers and accounting firms, but they may not have a deep knowledge of the intricacies of your business. You are the one with the day-to-day knowledge, so you need to understand how to direct procurement to help with the transaction.

Where does procurement sit in this hive of activity? Some may say 'on the sidelines', others would be willing to hear about it but not sure how they could help. Another group, a small group, sees the real value that procurement can bring but only when the function is mature by way of outstanding people and flexible, value-adding process.

Procurement may not be the first function that springs to mind when discussing M&A, but it doesn't mean it cannot offer quantifiable value. Procurement, strategic procurement that is, has the knowledge

---

1 Baiada Poultry 2007, viewed 3 November 2015,
http://www.baiada.com.au/news/Bartter%20Steggles%20Acquisition.html

and skills to enhance the process and amplify the financial benefits that can accompany a purchase.

Procurement's involvement should be across the three main stages of the acquisition process; target identification, due diligence preparation and integration.

IDENTIFY THE TARGET

Guy Haslehurst, former Director of Transaction Advisory Services at Ernst & Young and now CFO of Vics Premium Quality Meat has participated in and advised on numerous transactions in the private sector. Having observed both successful and unsuccessful bids, he has been able to see how procurement has and should be involved throughout the M&A process.

Acquisitions may be performed for any number of reasons, some of which could include security of supply, economies of scale, building market share, accessing new distribution channels or entering new markets. Whatever the reason there will be a direct or indirect impact on the supply base. It is for these reasons that Guy believes procurement should be involved during strategy formation—especially in the determination of possible synergies.

Generally, acquisitions are supported by a business case or investment thesis that is provided to the Board or Investment Committee. This outlines the strategic and financial reasons why the investment is desirable. Guy has observed instances where an acquisition decision, along with the predicted benefits, has been made without the engagement of procurement specialists. This increases the risk that the identified opportunities, may not be realisable and, as a result, there is a risk of overpaying for the asset.

Sometimes there is a disconnect between the strategic reasons for a purchase and the ability to execute decisions on the ground. If you can identify these risks early, it will ensure a greater likelihood of extracting the full value put forward in the business case.

The more detail included in determining the positive and negative, as well as the possible and probable impacts on supply, the better the chance that the forecast will be achieved.

DUE DILIGENCE

Right from the get-go, a polished and rigorous procurement professional can make significant contributions by leveraging their understanding of suppliers and supply chains.

Below are a handful of potential tasks that a strategic procurement function can fulfil in the lead up to an acquisition.

TASK

1. Identify, assess and categorise contracts (subject to access), spend segments and suppliers with the highest risk and commercial value. This allows for focus to be applied where it's needed most.

2. Quantify the existence of commitments, obligations (pricing or capital purchases) and strategic understandings with suppliers. Supplier due diligence is important as it allows all commitments to be aired that may prevent, limit or restrict activities.

3. Assess the pros and cons of change of control clauses in contracts and the ability to renegotiate, exit or novate them.

4. Analyse the inventory management models in use. Inventory analysis will help determine the exposure and commitments that might be in place with suppliers.

5. Clarify the size, structure and approach taken by the procurement team that is proposed to be acquired. Objectively compare their way of working against your own and prepare to adopt the best solutions and methods.

Well-run due diligence, in the case of a trade buyer/seller relationship, will allow for early identification of common ground and a clear priority of tasks to address once the transaction takes place.

By involving procurement from the outset, the likelihood of opportunities being overlooked are reduced, and the activity can begin in earnest after signing.

POST-ACQUISITION INTEGRATION

Before the ink has dried on a contract, two businesses find themselves joined at the hip, yet they are still operating as independent entities.

There are instances where businesses are purchased and are left to run independently. For the acquisitions that require integration, you need to examine what is involved, how procurement can help, and where it should all begin. Below are a number of actions that are worth consideration:

1. **Integration team:** Select a procurement integration team comprising staff from both businesses. There's no room for power plays—the combined team needs to pull together to achieve a melding of the businesses in the shortest possible timeframe.

2. **The new data set:** Recast a combined spend map of both businesses without delay, perform opportunity assessments and prioritise change by benefit, effort, and risk.

3. **Key suppliers:** Speak directly with the top suppliers from each company. Explain the change, outline the process, ask for cooperation and innovation. Look for the key supply relationships, strategies, technology and change programs that may already be in place and identify those suppliers that are willing to work with your business.

4. **Process:** Make sure your critical processes are standardised immediately. The Purchase-to-Pay process (Chapter 8) is a great place to start. You need to ensure suppliers are paid without disruption and there needs to be consistency, accuracy and efficiency in processes as soon as feasible.

5. **Contracts:** What contracts can be novated and should this be carried out? Is it better to maintain continuity of supply through novation or renegotiate the agreement? Be sure to adequately appraise the contractual position with suppliers without delay.

TREAD WITH CARE

Mergers are readily thought of as a great opportunity to rationalise and consolidate, reduce expense and make a company leaner. While this can be true, there are other considerations that need to be thought through before taking the knife to everything that looks like fair game.

1. **Plan carefully**

    It is easy to unwind something; it's much harder to rebuild it.

    I remember an instance where a particular manufacturing business identified that the culture within procurement was too deal-orientated, hostile with suppliers and lacking supply-derived innovation. The procurement manager was replaced and the new leader set about developing constructive, commercial relationships with suppliers. In response to this new direction, one key supplier invested heavily in a more innovative and relationally-minded team.

    In a turn of events, the manufacturing business was acquired. The new owners had a one-eyed view of their goods and services purchased—price. Little value was placed on innovation or the collaborative relationship formed. The program was mothballed within a few months. The supplier was forced to re-assign a price and margin-driven sales team to keep the account profitable, and successfully engage with its restructured and aggressive client.

    Twelve months later, when the manufacturer realised the benefits of the defunct program and tried to have it reinstated, the supplier pulled out. It was too great a drain on time and commercial resources to attempt to rebuild teams that suited this client.

2. **Ensure the savings are real**

    It's not unusual for savings to be identified at a strategic level. What commonly unfolds is that those who identified the savings take little responsibility for delivery. This is a disconnect that can have disastrous results.

It's not unless you are in the trenches of the business that the forecast figures can be quantified.

Procurement should be involved in the generation of the savings figure. This is a sure-fire way of making sure that the number is achievable since they will be the team who needs to deliver it.

Whether generated by consulting firms or derived from an in-house source, the depth of analysis for identifying savings figures must be comprehensive. Avoid making assumptions or run the risk of inflating savings values. A few traps to watch out for include:

- Historical volumes can be assumed to be indicative of future volumes and in some instances, serve as a forecast of company growth.

- Generalised benchmarked rates can be used to demonstrate a difference in price compared to current pricing paid. The challenge here is that the unique technical specification of some items may not be considered, and an 'apple for apple' comparison is not made.

- Savings can be derived from the consolidation of vendors and volumes to a single hypothetical supplier. When performed without consideration of the required technical capabilities or potential capacity constraints, forecast benefits may be unachievable.

My point in all this is simple. Have procurement validate the savings before pronouncing it from the rooftops. It's always embarrassing, and potentially career-limiting, to have to make an about-face.

3. **Which process to use**

Just because it is your process, doesn't make it the best.

Have an open mind and consider alternative approaches to everything from tendering, contract management, innovation extraction and stakeholder engagement.

Equally, the bigger entity in the transaction isn't always right. If procurement has an open mind to different approaches, it's amazing what can be improved along the way.

COMMERCIAL TIE-BACK

There are potential savings to be gained following a trade-to-trade transaction event.

Leveraging combined volumes to secure better pricing is the simplest of approaches. While this will yield fruit, be aware that some suppliers may not see eye-to-eye. They may already be supplying both businesses. Alternatively, they may push back on aggregated volumes, preferring to channel local volumes through local distribution points rather than global buying models.

What other significant commercial opportunities are available?

1. **People:** No one likes the job of carrying out redundancies. However, there will inevitably be a duplication of roles, and some positions may be made redundant. Headcount reduction and redeployment is one of the largest areas to find benefits, but make sure you don't prune too heavily too soon. Completing the merger well is important. If it is rushed and staff are made redundant too soon, it can be considerably harder to make the necessary changes.

2. **Technology and Innovation:** Acquisitions present a significant opportunity to gain legitimate access to the inner workings of another business and see what benefits suppliers are bringing. Make sure you don't let this chance pass you by. A collaborative approach with open communication channels will encourage more information sharing than may otherwise be experienced.

3. **Process:** Every business has a way of working to support primary operations. The Purchase-to-Pay process, payroll management, the financial month-end process, even logistics and warehouse handling process (to some degree) will all be present and managed differently. Difference is an opportunity. It allows for the testing of what works best. Make sure your team leaves their agenda at the door and brings a willingness to evolve and adopt improvements in the interest of progression.

TOP TIPS

1. If you have been through an acquisition event—was procurement involved? List the details where procurement performed well, what opportunities were missed and what could be improved. This can then be used as a basis for creating a structured plan with more effective procurement involvement for the future.

2. If you are looking to make an acquisition, it would be beneficial to develop a plan outlining how procurement can be involved early to assist with due diligence and planning.

3. Maybe you are looking to sell. Think how procurement can be involved to improve contracts, assets, supply innovation, efficiencies and processes to make your business a more attractive acquisition target.

CHAPTER 12

Intelligent Contracting

I was a young boy when my father opened his legal practice.

Despite his relative success, he retained the Australian knack for self-deprecation. Always with a joke or anecdote, he was happy to speak out loud what others regularly just thought. For instance: "What do you call one hundred lawyers at the bottom of the sea — a good start."

This was the type of dry humour that then and even now, makes me groan and yet somehow I relate to it.

It was the regular stories and jokes that made their way home from the office that allowed me to see first-hand just how important relationships were. Time and again, clients would return, not just because of the results my father would deliver but because of the rapport he had built.

Law, like procurement, can be a dry topic. Yet what brings them both to life is their common need to build constructive relationships and generate meaningful commercial outcomes.

I want to explore that association and outcome here.

PROCUREMENT AND LAW

For some time now, procurement has been working closely with the legal fraternity. Whether it be the management of external legal spend or collaborating to develop supply contracts, the two functions have become surprising associates.

How effective is this relationship in producing suitable contracts? That can often be answered by observing how a contract is used. Is it there to line a filing cabinet or lift the height of the computer screen? Or is the contract a powerful document that is used to help grow and progress your business?

For some companies, the generation of a contract is just a required part of the engagement process, and it is soon forgotten. Unless and until a problem raises its head or it's time for renewal. Thankfully, there is much more that can be done by procurement to help improve contract effectiveness.

CHANGE IS AFOOT

Warren Kalinko, CEO of Keypoint Law, describes how the legal landscape is changing. We're beginning to see a groundswell of differing approaches and models that make it easier for clients to select and engage a firm, secure greater value for money, develop constructive rapport and focus on the calibre of the lawyer rather than the company that employs them.

Warren described three trends that have emerged since 2005.

1. It's becoming increasingly common to find lawyers that have historically worked in large legal firms take on permanent legal counsel positions within private industry. Effectively, the sup-

plier now becomes the buyer, shifting the power from supplier to customer. This change has rewritten the rules for the procurement of legal services. Many companies are now highly conversant in understanding what legal advice is required, how it should be addressed and what the end outcome should be.

2. In forward-looking companies, procurement works collaboratively with in-house legal counsel. This relationship combines the knowledge of legal practice with the know-how of procurement process, structure, and negotiations, resulting in the development of more effective legal panels and importantly, contracts. This produces a better outcome than either function could have hoped to achieve independently.

3. There are a growing number of boutique legal firms, established by lawyers with a history from within larger legal practices. They can provide experience, knowledge, and expertise in a lighter, leaner offering with lower overheads and more personalised service. This is creating greater choice for the business community and allowing high-quality advice to be accessed that once would have been cost-prohibitive for many companies.

THE SIMPLE NEED FOR CONTRACTS

There was a time when business operated on a handshake. Those days seem to have passed, and it is becoming less common to find large companies with no supply agreements in place. This is not always the case with mid-sized organisations.

I remember helping a health industry supply company that sold goods with a limited shelf life. It had a significant turnover and yet no supply contracts could be found. When examining contractual arrangements with this company's customers, unsurprisingly, agreements were in place in almost every situation.

The exposure and risk regarding suppliers simply had not been considered. What if a supplier to my client provided an expired item that was then on-sold? They would have had few contractual levers with their supplier should their customer choose to pull out the contract and make a claim.

A similar example was with a supplier of lighting systems. It had a contract with a large national retailer, fitting out their stores within Australia. An agreement was in place between the retailer and the lighting specialist. However, no supply contract was in place between the lighting company and their suppliers. In the event the retailer made a warranty claim, and a component supplied to the lighting company was at fault, there was no contractual framework in place to manage this claim through the supply chain.

CONTRACTS AND BUSINESS GROWTH

Contracts don't always live up to their intended purpose. When this takes place, at best an agreement can be ineffective, at worst it can be highly damaging for an organisation.

In 2015, South African Airlines (SAA) engaged Ernst & Young (EY) to uncover why the airline was not profitable. In December that same year, having examined 48 contracts, EY provided the airline with a draft forensic report.[1] SAA made a statement that "The report shows that 28 of these 48 contracts (60 per cent) are improperly negotiated, poorly contracted or weakly managed". The report then went on to

---

1 Ferreira E, 2015, 'SAA's procurement woes exposed', *IOL*, 9 December, viewed 18 January 2016, http://www.iol.co.za/business/companies/saas-procurement-woes-exposed-1957743

described how these contractual weaknesses in the airline's procurement contracts may well be a cause for the airline's losses.

If that is an illustration of contractual failure, what about when it just hums? Behind every contract is a business case that a company wishes fulfilled. This is supported by a set of schedules, the parameters around what and why goods and services are being purchased in the first instance.

Warren Kalinko indicated that the critical question to ask at the outset of contract formation is:

"Will the contract achieve the business case? That is the fundamental question that every contract needs to be able to answer."

As Warren indicated, the answer lies in the contract schedules. Convention has it that lawyers may see this as the commercial realm of a contract with which they have no need to be involved.

While it's not the lawyers' responsibility to build the schedules, they do have a responsibility to understand the business case, what the contract is trying to achieve and whether the contract can deliver that purpose. If this is understood, an agreement can then be crafted to fulfil the business case that, in turn, will assist business growth.

By way of an example, if there is a component of an agreement that must be performed by a certain date, then it is critical for the lawyer to understand this requirement so that the contract is drafted to deliver this outcome. Early warning signals should be included in the agreement to give due notice in the event that the timeframe is at risk of not being met.

'OPERATIONALISATION' OF CONTRACTS

How often are contracts written, then put in the bottom drawer and never thought about again? All knowledge of the various rights, terms and structure designed to bring benefit to the business are grossly underused and effectively forgotten.

What if contracts could be massaged into documents that are easy to digest and subsequently, straightforward? They could be passed on from one individual to another as various people move through any given role.

This is possible and can be called the 'operationalisation' of contracts. Making a contract useable and functional for a business is the result.

The easiest way of achieving this is to distil the key elements of an agreement into a toolkit for effective management. Then, those that are impacted have an awareness of how to deliver the original business case. This toolkit may include things such as critical dates, pricing formulae, rebates, director's guarantees, novations, indemnities, obligations, and insurance—all the matters anyone new to the agreement would need to understand.

If the original contract has been well written, this toolkit should be able to be produced by procurement, for circulation to the relevant business managers.

CONSIDERATIONS

Contracts should be created to enable and encourage productive and profitable ways of working. If a contract's main reason for existence is to curb, control and correct, inevitably it won't be long before communications and relationships between the parties begin to breakdown. This is not a great start to a potentially multi-year partnership.

However, there are a few simple areas worth considering that help produce a mutually beneficial agreement and yes, procurement has a role to play:

1. Make sure the commercial elements are agreed upon before the contract is drafted. It is one thing to make changes to a term sheet pre-contract generation; it's a different, more expensive and time-hungry option to make changes after contract drafting. The lawyer should not start creating the agreement until after procurement has settled the contents and is clear on the intent.

2. Focus on dispute avoidance rather than dispute resolution. Disputes often arise out of how a contract's schedules may be interpreted and performed — this is where the work is defined in the first instance. It is far better to spend time upfront getting the schedules right and reduce instances of dispute rather than expensive and timely litigation where no party wishes to back down from their position.

3. Never play a zero-sum game. Liquidated damages, termination for convenience, one-sided indemnities and so forth — if they don't help deliver the end business case then their presence should be questioned. Clause inclusion needs to enable an agreement, not disable it. It will be challenging for procurement to create constructive supplier rapport if the legal instrument is framed around penalisation.

COMMERCIAL TIE-BACK

You'd struggle to find a successful business that was prepared to invest their finances without thorough analysis and investigation of the potential return.

Many of these commercial decisions will then go on to be wrapped up in a contract, and this is where consideration of the business case may end. Make sure to ask the question: how will this agreement support and enable the intended business direction?

In mid-market organisations, every cog needs to turn. Contracts that don't enable company growth and progression are taking the business backwards.

Procurement is one of the contributors to the contract generation process. It is the team that will understand the business case, will liaise with legal to produce an agreement, and will broker that final signoff with the supplier.

Provide the team with the table below as a start point for ensuring each and every contract supports the intended financial and operational direction of your business.

Forming the Business Case

Question	Response
1. What is the business hoping to achieve?	
2. How will a contract help deliver this outcome?	
3. What important elements must the contract contain to achieve the desired outcome?	
4. What commercial opportunities will become available by having a contract?	
5. What risks and lost opportunities may arise by not establishing a contract?	

TOP TIPS

1. Assess how procurement is currently involved in your contract generation process and how this could be improved through the 'operationalisation' of contracts.

2. Review how procurement can develop closer working relationships with in-house or external legal counsel and what commercial benefits this would bring.

3. For the top 20 suppliers in your business, have procurement expertise review the contractual status to access the effectiveness of existing agreements and commercial opportunities that may be available.

CHAPTER 13

Partner or Supplier

We've all had challenging customers. They increasingly expect more in quality, timeliness, and innovation, regularly expecting what we do to be delivered at the same or lower costs.

In some industries, FMCG particularly, deliveries can be turned away if only a few minutes outside of a delivery window and whole product lines can be delisted for a few consecutive failures in quality.

In my days of deodorants and laundry powder, ice cream and pasta sauce, The Trade—the large national grocery retailers—ran a pretty tight ship. They were on a path to increase quantities of their own private label, and they made their suppliers, Unilever being one, compete very hard to get a position on the shelf.

PARTNER TO WIN

Your suppliers are a linchpin. How can high-quality goods or services be provided to your customers if your suppliers are underperforming? Change is no small task, particularly when it may involve a fundamental shift in how a business works with suppliers. That was Unilever Australasia's realisation in the early 2000s.

Nowadays, Unilever has what has been coined 'Partner To Win'.[1] Started in 2011, it is a program that focuses on sustainability, innovation, quality, service, responsiveness and value. At the same time, it aims to develop mutually beneficial strategic supplier partnerships. What began as a procurement-led program with 200 of Unilever's global suppliers, it is now a way of working throughout the business.

Why are these partnerships highly valued? Unilever's ambition is to grow in size whilst reducing their environmental footprint and increasing positive social impact. When speaking to Dhaval Buch, Unilever's Global Chief Procurement Officer, he explained that this sustainable growth will only be possible with the involvement of suppliers.

Dhaval shared that Unilever looks at procurement-led partnerships as long-term, adaptable arrangements with multiple elements, not just transactional purchasing. Partnership frames the interaction—relationships are what bind it. If the notion of creating mutually beneficial relationships with scale and advantage was not there, then there would be little point to the partnership.

When asked what he sees as the mechanics of creating and sustaining supply partnership, Dhaval shared three elements:

1. **People**: Have the right people. Processes will follow what people do. People need experience and exposure to different parts of a business, so they understand the complexity of the company. This allows the team to talk business with a supplier, not just procurement.

---

1 Unilever 2016, *Supplier Centre—Partner to Win*, viewed 16 August 2015, https://www.unilever.com/about/suppliers-centre/partner-to-win/

2. **Governance**: Senior management must be involved in each partnership. There needs to be frequent interaction between these leaders to ensure the partnership is governed appropriately.

3. **Outcome Focused**: Partner To Win is an enablement program and like any other strategy, it needs to deliver results. The outcomes for Unilever have been agreeable, and the program has been continued and enlarged since 2011.

One of the striking remarks that Dhaval said was: "For our suppliers, we like to increase their business as we grow ours. The consequence—suppliers enjoy working with Unilever."

In many instances, Unilever develops the capability of suppliers, Dhaval explained, and then asks them to invest in (particular) markets. By their nature, these relationships are based on trust. Effectively, Unilever collaborates with suppliers for its own future requirements in a particular geography or industry, whilst encouraging the supplier to increase their own business and capability.

Although Unilever is a global business, the approach and principles of their Partner To Win program can be applied by mid-market companies. The easiest way of doing this is through your own fit-for-purpose Supply Relationship Management (SRM) program.

PROGRAM PURPOSE AND BENEFITS

SRM is a program targeted at suppliers who are critical to your business. The express intent is to encourage closer working relationships that deliver sustained improvements to business operations. Through the development of these supplier relationships, the program owner will frequently uncover opportunities to:

1. Work closer with suppliers to consolidate spend and minimise costs.

2. Gain access to innovation and technologies.

3. Gain first-to-market advantage.

4. Improve operating methods.

5. Minimise risk to supply. And perhaps...

6. Identify prospective acquisition targets.

On the other hand, the benefits for suppliers usually amount to integration into the customer's business and an increase in the quantity of goods and services purchased, due in part to a reduction in competition as well as fewer instances of open market tendering.

There is nothing better than first-to-market advantage or the ability to sustainably out-compete your competition on price and innovation. This is possible when the right relationship is struck between client and supplier. It comes down to how committed your business is to building a program that has cross-functional participation.

PROGRAM MANAGEMENT

Successful SRM starts from the top. While procurement is usually the program custodian, it requires CEO or Board buy-in.

This top-down endorsement of procurement's agenda 'encourages' other functions to participate. It also means suppliers can see that the whole company is behind the program, removing the pitfalls of a narrowly supported change program. This, in turn, increases the supplier's willingness to work with you.

Never underestimate the significance of business leadership participation. A public and frank sharing of performance, and disclosure of the challenges and opportunities ahead, is remarkably powerful. Explaining how the supply base can help goes a long way to encourage supplier participation.

If suppliers can see the authenticity of an SRM program, they will work exponentially harder to participate. Production facilities can be altered, purchasing practises changed and new innovation explored. When the credibility of a program is strong, the competition to be included will be equally robust.

I recall one instance where a supplier, of its own volition, provided its staff an incentive payment in the event that their business successfully retained a 'preferred' status on a SMR program.

As with all programs, there should be one driver but many passengers. Procurement frequently owns, manages and governs the program, but needs to acknowledge the contribution from other sections of the business including marketing, planning, operations, development, logistics, and payables.

Since the whole business is to be involved, there needs to be metrics that are publicly communicated. Agree upfront what success looks like, and then work out appropriate performance indicators that measure achievement and satisfaction. If you are looking for business buy-in, you need to demonstrate what their efforts are returning.

PROGRAM STRUCTURE

SRM in many respects is a program to prepare your business for the years ahead. It identifies those suppliers you really wish to work with for the longer term and encourages the whole business to draw together.

As with all activities in business, getting the structure right is important. Some considerations are listed below.

PROGRAM ENTRY

It is suggested that the program be cyclical in nature (e.g., annual) with regular review intervals. This means there is the prospect for new entrants and the removal of non-performing suppliers.

Not every supplier can or should participate—scarcity creates demand. A clear set of criteria should govern program entry. There needs to be rules around matters such as minimum spend thresholds, criticality of supply and performance metrics. These factors need to be openly disclosed and, importantly, upheld to maintain the integrity of the program.

SUPPLIER ASSESSMENT

The program should be able to assess and compare suppliers, irrespective of the industry they operate within, the size of the company or the goods and services supplied. This allows for a consistent comparison method between all suppliers.

Annual supplier rankings should be publicised. High performance needs to be recognised, and suppliers thanked for contributions made. This elevated profile has the effect of continued high performance from the winners and hunger to improve from those who missed out.

Have a structured plan to record, monitor, assess and deliver supplier workloads throughout the year. This program flourishes with regular engagement. Success is increased by having an accurate and central means of recording this information and the progress made.

INCENTIVISE

A balance between penalty and reward should be sought. Strong incentives for suppliers to perform rather than penalties for non-conformance are more effective at achieving sustained change. One such approach is to purposefully limit tendering activity.

Give program participants the first right of refusal for new work. Communicate with absolute clarity that assuming suppliers perform, remain cost-effective and innovate, there will be no need for the category to be tendered.

COLLABORATE AND COMMUNICATE

Be prepared to demonstrate how your company has skin in the game too. This could be displayed by:

- Time and expense invested by your business, as well as cross-functional participation.
- Provision of tools and templates for suppliers.
- Investing in suppliers to help them improve their operations.

Communication needs to be a two-way activity. Just as the program assesses a supplier's annual performance, the supplier needs to be encouraged, to share via annual reverse appraisal, how your business is performing. This is a priceless opportunity to hear openly from suppliers on how your business operates—without them fearing reprisal.

A WORLD WITHOUT SRM

Procurement within organisations that place little value on working with suppliers is often price-focused and deal-orientated. This doesn't sound like anyone's ideal client.

An executive manager (let's call him 'Adam') of a large labour hire business shared with me how in recent years his organisation walked away from several contracts worth multiple AUD$10's of millions each. Adam explained that over time, there had been an increasing focus from a handful of clients on price, with little interest in the value-adding services his business could bring. While these were large accounts, the margins were low and the time required to manage hostile clients brought the supplier relationship to a tipping point.

Ironically, Adam explained that his business then went on to have one of their better years since they had the capacity to pick up other accounts with better margins that valued and sought out their complementary services.

Businesses that take a hostile and price-focused approach can, in time, find themselves with limited supply options. Their narrow-sighted approach creates a reputation and consequentially a lack of appetite from some suppliers to engage.

TRAPS TO AVOID

No program is without pitfalls. Programs that are reliant on honesty, openness and goodwill do come with risks since people and agendas can get in the road. Be sure to consider the following as they will make for a smoother ride:

1. **Breaking the program rules.** If there are rules around entry, exit, tendering and so on, for goodness sake don't break them. If you do it once, you will do it again and then the integrity of the program is undermined. Why should suppliers trust you if you break the rules when it's convenient?

2. **Narrow company participation.** As SRM addresses the operations of business, the whole of the business needs to participate.

3. **No skin in the game.** If you're asking your suppliers to commit to your SRM program and let's face it, this is a reasonable commitment, you need to be able to show that it's 'costing' your business too.

4. **No supplier support.** If change is requested from suppliers, be prepared to help them out. In the end, it will benefit you.

In reality, some mid-sized businesses will have an SRM program in place. When this is the case, it is helpful to ask yourself:

- How effective is the program?
- How wide-spread is this way of working in the business? and
- How much of a cultural change has taken place?

Compared to the likes of a Unilever, a mid-market business may be relatively small. However, no matter the size, there are still opportunities to partner more effectively with suppliers and drive mutually beneficial outcomes. Every mid-market business has scale and leverage potential within the industry they operate. This is why procurement needs to be more than just a transactional function.

So if an SRM program would be of benefit to your business, what it comes down to is a change in mindset. Ask yourself: 'How do I grow beyond where I am right now?'

As Dhaval shared: "I am convinced this is the right model to create growth. No amount of internal capacity is ever going to substitute what's available out there with suppliers".

COMMERCIAL TIE-BACK

A supplier who has their services treated like a commodity will give you what you pay for—that can sometimes be below what you expect.

A supplier that you trust, who also trusts you, who earns a reasonable margin and can see a future in the business relationship will give you:

- Their best pricing and commercial terms
- Your choice of their resources
- Their knowledge and best thinking
- Speed of delivery
- Market analysis, trends, and innovation
- Collaborative incubators, and
- Help to resolve your challenges.

This results in increased speed, reduced error and the ability to meet the needs of your customers more effectively. The direct impact—increased business opportunities and revenue that otherwise may not have been possible. It's all brought together through a fit-for-purpose SRM program.

TOP TIPS

1. Consider how your business currently manages suppliers. Examine what it would take to enhance the performance of the supply base.

2. Evaluate which suppliers your business would benefit most through having closer ties. Consider what this relationship would look like and the possible result.

3. Should you decide to create an SRM program for your business, start by filling in the following table:

SRM Creation and Design

Consideration	Response
Program Objectives	
Entry Criteria	
Assessable Criteria	
Supplier Incentives	
Supplier Integration Methods	

CHAPTER 14

Brand and Credibility

BRAND

When we speak about brands, easily identifiable icons come to mind that may include clothing, food, cars and companies. What about the individual—do you have a brand as well?

Think back to earlier in your career. When you met someone for the first time, what would you feel when you told this person the name of your employer? Was it pride, indifference or a terrible sinking feeling? It's a company's brand that drives that response—what it stands for, its results and the people it employs. However, it is not only companies that have brands—people do too.

Your brand is your ambassador. What does it say about you or more importantly, what association is raised when others hear your name? Like it or not, people have an opinion of you, and they will be happy to share it. What they are speaking about is your brand.

I want to draw a distinction between reputation and brand.

Reputation is passive in nature. I describe it as the opinion others hold about you, formed as a consequence of the actions you take. Brand, however, is active in form; it's almost a verb. It's more than just your reputation; it's the continuous and deliberate process of creating an impression in the mind of others.

You can be very good at what you do and have an excellent reputation. However, your brand takes into account what you do and how you do it. It covers who you engage, what drives you, what you stand for, and what you value and believe in. It's not only limited to your work practises but is tested for consistency between your career and your personal life.

For most of us, our brand starts in obscurity — it's up to us if we stay there.

Condoleezza Rice was born in Alabama, the only child of a Presbyterian minister and teacher.[1] She grew up in colour-divided America, yet did not let her surrounding circumstances dictate her future. Consequentially, Rice went on to be the first African-American woman to serve as the U.S. National Security Adviser and U.S. Secretary of State.[2]

How is this relevant? Few of us have met Condoleezza Rice, even fewer know her personally, yet many will hold an opinion of her. Positive or negative, it doesn't matter as we still choose to form an opinion. It is her brand that we are considering—what she stands for, her values and how she conducts and projects herself, that's what we base our assessment on.

---

1 'Condoleezza Rice', *Wikipedia*, viewed 2 February 2016, https://en.wikipedia.org/wiki/Condoleezza_Rice.

2 United States Department of State—Office Of The Historian, *Biographies of the Secretaries of State: Condoleezza Rice (1954–)*, viewed 3 April 2016, https://history.state.gov/departmenthistory/people/rice-condoleezza

PROCUREMENT'S BRAND

Just like the company and the individual, each department has a brand as well. If the procurement team is staffed by individuals who are inexperienced and who hold a narrow view of what procurement can achieve, then the active message being broadcast is one of limited scope. In this instance, procurement is demonstrating that it is not equal to other business functions but is simply here to serve.

For many procurement professionals, advancing a career involves securing the right roles, skills, experience, contacts, and companies to work with. How regularly are the concepts and benefits of developing a personal brand addressed?

For any strategic change, time is required to plan and prepare for a deliberate shift in focus or change in approach. By cultivating an environment where the procurement brand is valued, a number of changes can take place.

1. **Staff Quality**: Competent and experienced professionals value the ability to provide genuine change and recognise the need for executive sponsorship. If the message portrayed is that the function is valued, a direct consequence will be the ability to attract higher-quality staff.

2. **Business Integration**: Greater levels of departmental integration is possible and probable when a clear message is issued from management that procurement is a material contributor to company progression.

3. **Supplier Performance**: The quality of your staff usually has a direct correlation with high-performing suppliers. Contract drift, poor service, and pricing fluctuations are common when suppliers are not managed well. A high-quality team will be able to draw out the best value from suppliers for the short and medium-term. Over time, industry recognises those businesses

that work well with suppliers. This creates competitive tension between suppliers to not only provide your goods and services but gain the right to say they work with your company.

Every individual has personal motivators that influence how their brand is displayed and perceived. The brand of each member of the procurement team is intrinsically linked to that of the department. Consequentially, the success or failure of the individual can have a material impact on the success or failure of the department.

Warren Kalinko, CEO of Keypoint Law, recognises the importance of the personal brand. He states: "It used to be that a client would choose a law firm based on the firm's brand. Increasingly, they're looking to choose the individual who has the expertise—regardless of the firm they're with. The decline in the importance of (*the*) firm(*s*) brand is being matched by the ascent of the personal brand."[3]

Our brand can be an individual's most precious professional resource. For procurement professionals to excel in their chosen field they can't afford to be vanilla; they can't apply the same rigid process delivering the same quantifiable results. They need to differentiate and develop an understanding of their business partners before their own immediate interests.

Procurement has a brand, as do the individuals in the department. How this is managed will determine the level of contribution that the department makes towards your business.

---

3 Kalinko, W 2014, 'Lawyers want a better deal', *Lawyers Weekly*, 21 October, viewed 23 April 2016, http://www.lawyersweekly.com.au/opinion/15831-lawyers-want-a-better-deal

CREDIBILITY

You wouldn't engage a plumber if they didn't know their trade. The same is true for procurement. Credibility demonstrates competence, differentiates an individual and team and builds stakeholder comfort before work even begins. Do those who manage procurement within your business demonstrate the below?

KNOWLEDGE AND ADAPTABILITY

Every professional must be able to demonstrate a thorough knowledge of their chosen field. The reality is, business takes the knowledge of a professional as assumed, and so they should. Just as we expect the plumber to know their way around pipes and fixtures and a neurosurgeon to understand the brain, procurement's internal stakeholders expect a demonstration of technical skill, business understanding, and commercial foresight.

What is valued more than knowledge alone is adaptability. The frustration of many internal stakeholders is procurement rolling-out rigid, process-driven programs that have questionable value. If procurement wants to be included in broader business decision-making and be seen as the go-to point for a particular group of skills, then the department must work towards becoming business partners, not simply service providers.

PROFESSIONAL STANDARDS

Procurement must be diligent and maintain the highest professional practice at all times. Failure to do so is effectively flushing personal and departmental brands down the drain.

While fraud and theft are intolerable, areas that might be deemed 'grey' are equally unacceptable. It should be the aim of every professional to stay clear of questionable practices, and not see how close they can get. To illustrate the point, below are a few 'grey' activities that procurement would do well to avoid:

- Willfully breaking contractual payment terms by delaying supplier payment to the next fiscal period, just to make the books appear more favourable.

- Claiming year-on-year savings without seeing a change in price within the contractual term.

- Issuing a tender with more favourable historical volumes that are known to not represent future trends.

- Claiming savings on forecast activities that are not expected to eventuate.

If slight distortions and shades of grey are tolerable, procurement will irrevocably damage its credibility and erode its brand. It's a slippery surface once an individual progresses down that path.

The vast majority of procurement practitioners seek to be respected for their work and valued by their business. While technical expertise and industry knowledge are important, an individual's ability to understand their personal brand and maintain credibility is the hallmark of any professional.

COMMERCIAL TIE-BACK

The success or failure of mid-market procurement will rest on the ability and experience of the individuals employed. Not so much their technical procurement skills but rather the strength of their brand and the degree of their credibility.

Business professionals who take pride in their work and value their craft are the individuals needed to drive change. Work is performed faster; results delivered sooner, and stakeholders are more thoroughly engaged. Flowing on from this, solutions become more flexible, and suppliers are better managed. Consequently, contributions can be made to areas conventionally out of reach for procurement.

Imagine that you have a team of five in procurement. Let's assume that a polished professional was able to complete work 10 per cent faster, save 5 per cent more, uncover three more initiatives each year, achieve 20 per cent more buy-in from the business per project, and help suppliers be 5 per cent more efficient.

What would this one individual mean to your business in raw commercial terms?

What would this mean to your business if two or more of the team could deliver this improvement? Try completing the table below:

The 'Effective' Operator

Benefits	Commercial Outcome
10% faster completion of work	
5% more savings p.a.	
3 more improvement initiatives p.a.	
20% more stakeholder buy-in per project	
5% more efficiencies with suppliers	

TOP TIPS

1. Consider how procurement's brand is actively promoted within your business.

2. With regards to its capability, contribution potential and insight for growth and profit, identify what message procurement should communicate to your business.

3. Consider the requirements to transform procurement's brand and credibility in your company to equal that of a strategic business partner.

CHAPTER 15

Boom and Bust

Business behaviours can change with the seasonality of an industry. The way companies operate when business is thriving can be very different compared to when times are tough. Quite often procurement's role can rapidly evolve—however, is this the best approach?

An open acknowledgement of how procurement's role can change through seasons was in a 2015 advertorial for a mining and procurement conference in Australia. The advertorial mentioned:

"2014 was a challenging year for the mining sector, and the outlook for 2015 is predicted to be around cost optimisation and 'doing more with less…'. During the boom time, many procurement practices were thrown out of the window, but during slower times processes need to be tightened up and improved upon."[1]

The role that procurement plays in any company is largely driven by what the executives believe procurement is capable of delivering and what it should contribute toward. The challenge to overcome is that businesses are limited by what they know. So I ask you, is the percep-

---

1 Conferize, *Mining Procurement & Supply APAC 2015*, viewed 18 May 2015, https://www.conferize.com/conferences/mining-procurement-and-supply-apac-2015/about

tion of procurement's capability and contribution limiting the benefit that the function could bring to your company through changing fiscal cycles?

Process and control are needed in every business to varying degrees. When the process becomes more important than the outcome or when the controls become a greater priority than the ability to enable business, this is when procurement has lost its way.

For procurement to contribute most significantly in both boom and bust, companies should avoid the swinging pendulum of it being in and out of favour, depending on the season. Opportunistically leveraging the function for all the wrong reasons will not lead to success.

BOOM TIMES

Large profits, a premium product, and high demand are some of the characteristics of businesses when they are riding a boom wave. When business is thriving, there is normally one of two approaches that companies adopt with regards to procurement:

1. Expand procurement's reach so that it contributes further initiatives that deliver additional growth and profit.

2. Make procurement of little consequence. An approach that some in the mining industry in Australia took in the boom years (circa 2010) as procurement was seen as a profit inhibitor through undue process.

While it is important for every business to extract the most from buoyant markets, we need to ensure that value-adding work is not thrown out in the interest of fast profits. What approaches could your business consider to draw maximum value from procurement?

1. **Indicators**

   Use the time to develop strategies for the downturns; good times don't last forever.

   Let me emphasise, there is a need to understand your key market indicators and markers. Recognising the signals for a turning of the tide back to a declining market is key.

   Whether it's foot traffic through a store, declining purchases of particular items or the softening of the sale of services commonly supplied to a buoyant market, procurement needs to recognise the signals and be able to develop a response.

2. **Top Line Performance**

   We know that procurement can make contributions to profit through savings, but what about revenue through sales? While the function is not usually at the heart of a sales transaction, it can enable those functions that are.

   Armed with advance knowledge of what is being developed, promoted, and sold, procurement can identify and groom relevant suppliers so that they will provide your business with the necessary goods and services for today and tomorrow's market initiatives.

   Procurement has to be seen by the business to play in the broader supply and value chain. There needs to be a deliberate move away from the notion that the function simply buys things (no matter if tactical or strategic). Instead, procurement should work with operations and sales to improve process and market penetration, a far cry from the negotiation of unit pricing for goods and services.

   Let's consider this from another perspective. Is your procurement team only privy to demand and supply planning data? In other words, they only hold scant knowledge of sales activity and promotional negotiations. If this describes your business, it's a pretty big gamble that your supply needs will be met when those responsible for sourcing goods and services operate blind to the strategic top line objectives.

3. **Supplier Relationships**

Boom times are when procurement should be investing in constructive supplier relationships. Build the trust, involve the suppliers, work collaboratively and they will be more likely to be there for you when you need them.

Procurement's aim should be to demonstrate a broad understanding of business and how its interactions with suppliers can improve operations, bring efficiency gains and introduce new technology and innovation. This is a far more compelling value proposition than being the function that 'buys'.

4. **The Entrepreneur Inside**

Encourage an entrepreneur mindset among the procurement team. Don't let them be crippled by imagination failure. Calculated risk should be encouraged with appropriate levels of transparency and safety nets, so the team is not burned by less-successful attempts at innovation and change.

A friend of mine within investment banking circles shared how it is a prerequisite for every individual within his business to demonstrate efficiency and improvement to the role they occupy, if they wish to be promoted. The subsequent culture is one of novel thinking and calculated risk, importantly, supported by executive management.

Encourage the natural and organic growth of ideas. Whilst the creation of entirely new product lines is exciting, their development, testing and marketing can be extensive and costly.

Perhaps an easier option is to encourage the team to expand upon what already exists and sells. The enhancement of proven and successful goods and services to retain ongoing relevance with customers stands to generate faster traction and greater returns.

THE SEASON OF BUST

My family has a long history with the land. Originating in Queensland as sugar cane farmers, they moved to NSW in the early 1900's with crops and cattle. I feel fortunate to have been able to spend many of my holidays as a boy with cousins and motorbikes, livestock and country homesteads. I look back on those years with fond memories but I know it can be a very different story for those who call life on the land home.

Drought is the single greatest sustained natural hardship that farmers have to face. Fire and flood can be catastrophic but they are short and sharp and allow you to move quickly into recovery mode. Drought, however, can go for years and years.

A family takes pride in building up the bloodline of livestock over decades. When this is wiped out by drought, it can destroy a farmer.

It starts with maybe a season or two of little to no rain; crops fail, and weeds take over. Livestock are hand-fed, and dams within paddocks begin to dry out. Soon even the weeds won't grow, and water needs to be trucked in. Livestock stop breeding, the old and young perish and for those remaining, their physical condition deteriorates.

The heart-wrenching job of shooting your own beasts then begins unless you can destock by freighting them to another property or selling them at the sale yards where the only buyer may be the slaughterhouse. Generations of breeding can end up on the butcher's hook.

Australian farmers are a hardy bunch, many do hang on until the rains return. Dams are filled, crops begin again and livestock once more flourishes.

As drought is to farmers, economic downturn is to the business community.

We all face our 'droughts'. How a business responds is largely determined by what they have done in the preceding years.

DEFEND OR GROW

A company's response to hard times is often one of either looking at what's done best, getting small, cleaning the 'shop' and focusing on process and efficiencies. An alternative approach for those companies that have prepared in advance is to take the opportunity and buy undervalued yet high-quality businesses.

Merger and acquisition activity is never going to be consistent. *Fortune Magazine* for instance reported global deal activity up 47 per cent or US$3.5 trillion between 2013 and 2014.[2] Likewise, Herbert Smith Freehills outline in their *Australian Public M&A Report 2014* that FY14 represented a larger surge of M&A activity in Australian markets than the preceding years.[3] Excluding private deals, there were 77 public ASX listed deals announced, valued at almost AUD$44 billion. Interestingly, the same report in 2015 demonstrated a contrac-

---

2 Primack, D 2015, '2014 was a huge year for M&A and private equity', *Fortune*, 5 January, viewed 16 June 2015,
http://fortune.com/2015/01/05/2014-was-a-huge-year-for-ma-and-private-equity/

3 Herbert Smith Freehills 2016, *Herbert Smith Freehills 2014 Australian Public M&A Report—M&A on the rise*, viewed 2 May 2016,
http://www.herbertsmithfreehills.com/insights/legal-briefings/herbert-smith-freehills-2014-australian-public-ma-report-ma-on-the-rise

tion of activity, down to only 55 deals in the 12 months to 30 June 2015.[4]

While it's great to be in the strong position to be able to buy other companies, not all businesses have these opportunities. So how could procurement respond?

WEALTH MANAGEMENT IN THE GFC

The Global Financial Crisis (GFC) was a gut-wrenching experience for many in business. In Australia alone, more than 30,000 of the most vulnerable of businesses shut their doors between the federal elections of 2007 and 2010.[5] A contact of mine held a leadership role within wealth management at this time and shared her experiences at surviving this financial horror.

Wealth management was hit harder than banks. At the time, the profit model was made up of fees as a proportion of funds under management. When the ASX index was falling at five percent per month cumulatively, wealth funds were literally watching revenue walk out the door.

Costs needed to be curtailed. There was, however, an acute awareness that if you simply took the unsophisticated approach and slashed 10 per cent of all expenses (this normally being payroll), would the business have the means to rebound when the tide turned?

---

4 Herbert Smith Freehills 2016, *Australian Public M&A Report 2015*, viewed 2 May 2016, http://www.herbertsmithfreehills.com/insights/issues/australian-public-m-and-a-report-2015

5 news.com.au, *Australia shuts up shop: the effect the GFC has had on your local stores*, May 16 2011, viewed June 3 2016, http://www.news.com.au/finance/work/australia-shuts-up-shop-malcolm-farr-on-the-effect-the-gfc-has-had-on-your-local-stores/story-e6frfm9r-1226056709832

The response was simple but highly effective. Projections of a continuing fall in the index by five percent per month were modelled. Overlaid here was what the cost-base needed to be to maintain margin and profit.

Various responses for each subsequent drop in the index were identified and grouped into tranches of actions that increased in severity the further the index fell. This approach prevented drastic and hard to reverse action being taken immediately instead, mapping out a plan for how the business would respond with each successive decline in the index.

The business was then able to understand what would be done at each trigger point, how quickly the action could be implemented, the degree of expense reduction the action would contribute and how deeply it would affect the organisation's ability to recover.

PROACTIVE OR REACTIVE

Undoubtedly there is a need to make changes to retain profit in tight times. However, there has to be resistance to dissolving the substance that defines strong procurement—high-quality teams, supply relationship, and innovation.

In simple terms; consolidate, simplify, standardise and innovate.

Below are five practical tips for procurement to undertake when times are lean. The overarching message is to explore alternative solutions before tossing everything away:

1. Develop a program with staggered cost-savings initiatives. Initiatives will increase in severity over time in order to help maintain margin and profitability.

2. Revisit previously shelved savings or revenue-generating projects. Consider if now is the time to implement these projects that may have previously been considered too hard or a lower priority.

3. Review vital back-end process. Ensure consistency throughout the business, remove duplication, increase adoption levels and resolve recalcitrant behaviour.

4. Draw upon the skills of suppliers. Explore a supplier's alternate services for improvements in cost and yield. Maintain supplier relationships; be open and honest about company performance and trends.

5. Review, report and implement all potential improvements for the company's products and services that generate the greatest profit.

COMMERCIAL TIE-BACK

Whilst you may not be able to control the market, you can take preparatory steps in readiness for a change in economic season. To not do this is to choose to bob about in the current and hope that you stay afloat.

The problem with deferring to chance is that some solutions are created in response to circumstance, rather than being a consequence of your strategy.

Ill thought through business planning runs the risk of being near-sighted and while it may appear sweet today, can turn sour tomorrow. For instance, a knee-jerk reaction to slash staff numbers and squeeze suppliers to the bone for a fast injection of cash will rarely turn out to be beneficial in the long run.

Instead, operate out of a position of strength. In any given season, have advanced knowledge of what could be done. When a business is able to select a response from pre-established options, that's when you can truly capitalise on market conditions.

This line of thinking signifies a number of things.

- You know what to action and when.
- You understand the impact on margin.
- You are aware of which actions are mild/conservative and what is severe/progressive.
- You understand the benefits it will bring and challenges that may arise.
- You know how long it will take to recover and how quickly gains will be made.

This approach is proactive. It is defensible.

The likelihood of sustained results is now dramatically increased.

TOP TIPS

1. What indicators exist in your business and industry that may signal the onset of a downturn?

2. Review your forward-looking procurement plan and consider how it could be improved. If there is no plan, consider how one could be structured to improve the speed and effectiveness of expense, vendor, contract and project management.

3. How does your business respond in seasons of boom and bust? Using the following table, consider what could be done to prepare for market upswings and declines.

The Boom and Bust Response

Planned Response for Boom	Planned Response for Bust

PART 5

A Promising Future

CHAPTER 16

Preparing for Tomorrow

WHAT LIES AHEAD

When you're forward planning for your business, what time frame do you project out to—five years, perhaps 10 years, or even 20 in some instances?

Medtronic, the multi-billion dollar medical devices company best known for producing half the world's pacemakers, was founded in 1949 with a 100-year business plan.[1] Just try and fathom that for a moment. Having scratched down a few ideas for maybe the next few years, you fast-forward into the realm of trying to imagine things that don't yet exist, then developing applications based on these figments of your imagination, and this is all before you get to the stage of making improvements to these processes.

Impossible you say. Not quite but such forward thinking requires extensive knowledge of an industry and bucket-loads of creativity. This is what Earl Bakken, the founder of Medtronic, had.

---

1 Mann, B 2000, 'Medtronic's Hundred-Year Business Plan', *The Motley Fool,* 19 May, viewed 3 February 2015,
http://www.fool.com/news/foth/2000/foth000519.htm

Planning for the development and maturity of procurement is no different (although perhaps we don't need a 100-year plan).

While the present can't be ignored, growth will be challenging to deliver without lifting our gaze beyond the present and recognising what is looming up in front of us. Just as the business leader sets the overarching objectives, the functional head needs to be able to come up with the mechanics on how this will be delivered, and procurement needs to contribute here.

If asked, where do you see yourself in the next 10 years, what would you say? You don't need to have the full-colour picture but an outline is essential. We need to aspire to something that does not yet reflect today's reality.

The same is true for the procurement function. What does your procurement function look like today? Where does it need to be for tomorrow? What would truly make it remarkable?

CHANGE AFOOT

Change in business and technology is faster today than ever before. If we don't keep up, we will be left behind.

The last few decades of the 20th century was when automation really took off, and many blue-collar roles became redundant as machinery was able to perform the same tasks faster for less.

White-collar roles and responsibilities are rapidly evolving too. If it can be automated, it will. If it can be disrupted, it'll happen.

For instance, in the legal arena, contracts can be generated automatically through cloud-based clause libraries. In health care, physiotherapy diagnosis, treatment, and monitoring can be performed through web-based technologies. The month-end accounting consolidation process has changed as well; some companies are able to close off their books with the click of a button.

In an interview with ABC's *7.30 Report* in August 2015, Professor Hugh Durrant-Whyte from the University of Sydney indicated that there is a high probability that 40 per cent of jobs will disappear within the next 10 to 15 years, due to automation and digital disruption.[2] Everything from booking a holiday to providing financial advice, these service jobs are the ones that are automatable now.

He should know. It was technology developed by the University of Sydney that fully automated Australia's Port Botany in 2015, having automated the Port of Brisbane just a few years earlier. The consequence: both ports now require fewer workers on the waterfront.

Procurement is not immune. Much of the process applied is on a collision course with automation, everything from tenders, panel selection, contract creation, and vendor assessment. The transactional and manual buying of things will fast become obsolete, and soon only strategic roles will remain.

Far from being an alarmist, this is an observation of what has been taking place over recent years. Routine tasks and roles with repetitive functionality are ever increasingly becoming exposed. It's the people focused, technically competent and innovation driven individuals that will thrive in this era of rapid change.

2 *7.30 hosted by Leigh Sales* 2015, television broadcast, 'Is your job going to disappear in the digital revolution?' Australian Broadcasting Commission, 25 August, reported by Matt Peacock, http://www.abc.net.au/7.30/content/2015/s4300018.htm

'TOMORROW'S DIGITALLY ENABLED WORKFORCE'

In March 2016, Australia's Commonwealth Scientific and Industrial Research Organisation (CSIRO) released their findings from a study that considered possible futures for jobs and employment markets up until 2035. This work culminated in a report, *'Tomorrow's Digitally Enabled Workforce—Megatrends and scenarios for jobs and employment in Australia over the coming twenty years'*.[3]

The work identified six megatrends. It was suggested that these gradual yet significant change factors will reshape business and employment markets over the coming twenty years.

3 Hajkowicz, S, Reeson, A, Rudd, L, Bratanova, A, Hodgers, L, Mason, C & Boughen, N 2016, *Tomorrow's Digitally Enabled Workforce: Megatrends and Scenarios for jobs and employment in Australia over the coming twenty years*, Commonwealth Scientific and Industrial Research Organisation (CSIRO), Brisbane, Australia.

Tomorrows Megatrends

Megatrend	Overview
The Second Half of the Chessboard	Rapid advances in automation and artificial intelligence mean that robotic devices can perform many tasks more quickly, safely and efficiently than humans. Yet change and growth are not expected to be linear. Progressing beyond 2020 (the second half of the chessboard), this is when rapid transformation is expected.
Porous Boundaries	The peer-to-peer economy is expanding. Jobs of the future and the businesses that provide them are likely to be more flexible, agile, networked and connected.
The Era of the Entrepreneur	The ideal job may not be ready and waiting for future job seekers. Instead, individuals both inside and outside large organisations will require entrepreneurial skills and aptitudes to create their own roles.
Divergent Demographics	Many economies have ageing populations with growing life expectancies. An organisation's workforce employee profile is expected to change to contain more diverse age groups and cultural backgrounds.
The Rising Bar	Increased use of automation means that higher skills for entry-level roles are required. In spite of this, the soft skills gap will need to be bridged. There is a growing demand for individuals who possess appropriate interpersonal and organisational awareness skills.
Tangible Intangibles	Employment growth in service industries is likely to continue as a move toward a knowledge economy speeds up. Service sector jobs requiring skilled social interaction and emotional intelligence will become increasingly important.

Dr Andrew Reeson is an applied economist who works with Data61, a team within CSIRO. He is also the co-author of *Tomorrow's Digitally Enabled Workforce*.

When we spoke, Andrew shared some remarkable insights on where society is headed.

Que: What trends are taking place within white-collar professions?

Ans: There has been a steady upskilling of the highly capable professional whilst an increasingly steep decline in the demand for blue-collar professions and lower skilled white-collar roles—bookkeepers and analysts for instance.

Automation is driving this change. Routine tasks are being heavily automated, and conventional roles are disappearing. That spells opportunity for the more skilled individual. Accountants, lawyers, medical practitioners, perhaps even strategic procurement can now do more, faster and with less help.

It was interesting to find that the commercially minded, forward looking, innovation focused and relationally driven skill sets are increasingly in demand. These are the attributes that are shaping employment for the future.

Que: What is driving this disruptive way of working?

Ans: Disruption is only going to increase. In other words, the creative process of using technology to find new ways to re-create existing business models, industries, and social interaction is just in its infancy.

There is a growing interest to challenge how business has been previously conducted. It's not always about finding a new niche but rather using technology to create new solutions to old business models.

Two commercial reasons for the interest in disruptive technologies are the potential for a reduction in the cost of doing business and scalability.

Once the front-end cost of technology and design has been accounted for, the marginal cost of a digital product is reduced to almost $0. Care should be taken since a highly replicable digital product might look attractive, however because the cost per serve is so low, the price sold can approach that same figure. It just takes someone to give the product or service away for industries to immediately struggle.

Scalability is another driver. Having a digital product or service can make the opportunities almost limitless. Take Amazon for instance; you could argue that the cost per serve would be very low, yet the returns to scale are almost limitless. This makes it very difficult for any other business to compete if they don't have digital products and services or lack a genuine point of difference.

Que: How could changing technology impact employment trends?

Ans: Jobs most susceptible to automation are those that can be considered routine and have well-defined rules and structures. These are highly suited to codification. By breaking jobs down into their component tasks and activities, it's possible to estimate how susceptible a role is to automation.

'*Tomorrow's Digitally Enabled Workforce*' showed that people-type skills have had the strongest growth or employment demand. Individuals who can work with both customers and stakeholders will be best suited to this changing environment.

The ideal future worker will be utterly fluent in technology, yet does not try to be the technology. They will be able to relate and interact with others using a high degree of professionalism and interpersonal insights.

The technology will continue to evolve whether we like it or not, whether we adopt it or not. What business really needs is the right type of team to effectively use technology while growing and developing stakeholder rapport. I'd suggest that business doesn't need its workforce to become computing experts rather, employ and engage capable individuals who use technology to their advantage without it being detrimental to important commercial relationships. In other words, let technology sort out process and allow people to engage people.

Que: What should a mid-market company do to prepare for change?

Ans: It's important to consider how technology can change the way business is carried out rather than just thinking of it as a way to reduce cost. The essential consideration revolves around discovering new ways of working, new markets, new business models and products.

One of the ways to do this is to examine different business platforms or models. In other words, a way to create or tap into an electronic marketplace that brings together suppliers and clients. New ways of doing business better are where the real disruption have and will continue to occur.

Take Uber for instance; in its simplest form, it changed the business model of the taxi industry. It tapped into smartphone capability (that was not made with this application in mind), linking online booking functionality with drivers. The product is arguably the same—someone is driving someone else around town. It's the business model that is completely different.

Automation should be the other focus. Organisations need to consider where in their business process, whether carried out by human or machine, automation can be achieved. And for the ride-sharing industry, the driverless Uber could well be an example of automation for the next generation of service.

A BRIGHT FUTURE

Below are several examples of disruptive technologies and business practices that are set to make significant changes within business.

As you progress through, think how your procurement team is currently or could potentially contribute. Of the relevant technologies, does procurement understand them? Are they working with sales, marketing and development on how to use and position your business with these advancements? What discussions are taking place with suppliers on how to progress forward?

Remember, procurement should be engaging suppliers, understanding advancements and helping your business position itself to capitalise on emerging trends. This may be a step change from existing methods of contribution but as the conventional custodian of suppliers, it would be remiss of procurement not to be up to speed on technology and supplier capability.

3D PRINTING

While not a new technology (in fact 3D printing has been around for decades but only made its first commercial appearance in 2009), it has now been made widely available due to lower barriers to entry.[4]

---

4 3D Printing Industry 2016, *History of 3D Printing: The Free Beginner's Guide*, viewed 3 February 2015,
http://3dprintingindustry.com/3d-printing-basics-free-beginners-guide/history/

For as little as a few thousand dollars, the general public can purchase a 3D printer while the technology extends up to full-size industrial machines. As *Forbes Magazine* explains: "prototyping continues to dominate the reasons why enterprises pursue 3D printing, with the opportunity of improving new product development and (reducing) time-to-market being long-term goals."[5]

This technology means that many parts and components, historically purchased from a third party, can now be produced in-house. Gone is the need for keeping certain lines of inventory. Enter the new definition of vertical integration where in-line component manufacturing is set to become a part of the overall product creation process.

A number of industries are on a collision course with this technology—logistics and warehousing being examples. The demand for freighting and storage services is set to decline with a growing capability for business to produce what is needed on-site.

Wohlers Associates have been tracking the 3D printing industry since the 1980s. Its analysis, *Wohlers Report 2014* (as featured in an article published by the investment services firm, The Motley Fool) paints a compelling picture.[6] While this is still a relatively small industry, the projected growth is reported to be considerable. The value of the global industry is recorded at US$3.07 billion in 2013 and forecasts revenue to be US$12.8 billion in 2018 and US$21 billion worldwide by 2020.

---

5 Columbus, L 2015, '2015 Roundup Of 3D Printing Market Forecasts And Estimates', *Forbes*, 31 March, viewed 3 April 2015,
http://www.forbes.com/sites/louiscolumbus/2015/03/31/2015-roundup-of-3d-printing-market-forecasts-and-estimates/#162675461dc6

6 Heller, S 2014, 'Why 3D Printing Stocks Could Have a Tremendous Runway for Growth', *The Motley Fool*, 9 September, viewed 3 February 2015,
http://www.fool.com/investing/general/2014/09/09/why-3d-printing-stocks-could-have-a-tremendous-run.aspx

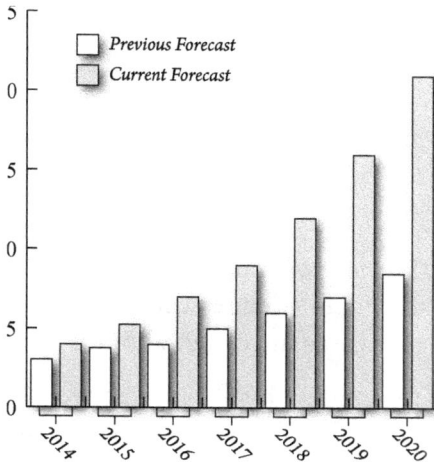

Worldwide 3D Printing Industry
Forecast, Billions.
Source: The Motley Fool[7]

SOURCES OF PROTEIN

There's no denying that the world is moving East. With the rise of China and growing wealthy middle-class in SE Asia, these populations are moving away from a diet of cereals to one that has higher protein content.

Conventional protein sources have been red and white meat, fish and some plants. There is a growing movement to source food stocks from less conventional means—insects and lab-cultured meat.

---

7 Heller, S 2014, 'Why 3D Printing Stocks Could Have a Tremendous Runway for Growth', *The Motley Fool*, 9 September, viewed 3 February 2015, http://www.fool.com/investing/general/2014/09/09/why-3d-printing-stocks-could-have-a-tremendous-run.aspx

While your skin may crawl at the thought of eating a cricket or cutting up a steak that has been grown in a lab, we have to acknowledge that our rate of land use and population growth will make current food consumption practices difficult to sustain. When faced with this scenario, alternative food sources need to be considered.

An article in the online publication *Food Navigator* speaks of these emerging trends. Charles Spence, head of the Crossmodal Research Lab at Oxford University acknowledges that insects would become a mainstream food source but was uncertain about when.[8]

In late 2014, food safety guidelines for insects were created for the first time in response to their likelihood of being grown, harvested and eaten at scale. The Federal Agency for the Safety of the Food Chain (FASFC) in Belgium released the guidelines citing more than 2000 known edible insect species.[9] The agency acknowledged that there is still little scientific literature available on the subject. While commercial operations are a way off, these alternatives are now firmly on the food industries' radar.

In 2013, Dr Mark Post of the University of Maastricht in the Netherlands presented the first lab-cultured beef hamburger.[10] Muscle cells are painlessly harvested from a living cow. These cells were then fed and multiplied to create muscle tissue—the main component of the

---

8 Daniells, S 2014, "Innovation in product development and formulation is needed for insects to emerge as a mainstream food source': UN advisor on edible insects', *FoodNavigator-asia.com*, 18 February, viewed 3 February 2015,
http://www.foodnavigator-asia.com/Markets/Innovation-in-product-development-and-formulation-is-needed-for-insects-to-emerge-as-a-mainstream-food-source-UN-advisor-on-edible-insects

9 Robinson, N 2015, 'First EU edible insect food safety guide published', *FoodNavigator-asia.com*, 28 January, viewed 3 February 2015,
http://www.foodnavigator-asia.com/Nutrition/Europe-s-first-insect-food-safety-guide

10 Cadwalladr, C 2014, 'Laboratory-grown beef: meat without the murder, but would you eat it?', *The Guardian*, 13 July, viewed 3 February 2015,
https://www.theguardian.com/science/2014/jul/13/laboratory-grown-beef-meat-without-murder-hunger-climate-change

meat we eat. The output was a cultured product that is biologically identical to the meat tissue from cattle.

The benefits of cultured vs. paddock originating meat include 99 per cent less space needed and production of far less greenhouse gas emissions.

Other positive environmental consequences from the technology may include solutions for long-held challenges such as Japan's taste for whale meat. Alternate sources of protein will continue to be significant areas of discussion, disruption, and development.

While many companies battle with 'green' credentials, sustainable sources of food, ethical use of overseas labour and the growing need to control emissions, these solutions provide a new level of possibility. If you are in the food industry, how is your procurement team coming to terms with these potential applications? Do they have the necessary sources of supply for the delivery of low-risk yet high-quality solutions?

COLLABORATIVE ECONOMIES

The concept is simple: in collaborative economies, consumers are able to get what they need from each other without having to rely upon large organisations as a source. Business is now catching on and adopting a similar approach as well.

Jeremiah Owyang from Crowd Companies, an innovation council for large companies to unlock the collaborative economy, suggests this notion has filtered into many sectors of business. Jeremiah describes how collaborative economies exist across services, transportation, space, money, goods, food and more.[11]

Services are an interesting area. There are a number of businesses that are structured to serve as vast connectors of professional services to consumers globally. Upwork and 99designs are two such companies. A small start-up or large multinational can source either an individual graphic designer or perhaps an entire pre-vetted marketing and research team to develop solutions to a range of challenges.

GE is an example of a company taking a progressively different approach. It understands that breakthroughs can be achieved faster by using the greater collective power of talent through crowdsourcing projects. No longer relying on in-house talent alone or only going to one services company for solutions, GE takes its challenges to the 'global brain' to discover outcomes from individual entrepreneurs, boutique agencies and institutions.[12]

These are non-conventional supply sources. Nevertheless, the knowledge and skill of high-quality procurement can be brought to bear to help businesses scope, select and deliver the desired end result.

INTRA-INDUSTRY CROSS-POLLINATION

If procurement is (or should be) the custodian of relationship generation and management, then we need to throw the net wider. We need to move beyond what we know and grow again.

---

11 Morgan, J 2014, 'Why the Collaborative Economy is Changing Everything', *Forbes*, 16 October, viewed 3 February 2015,
http://www.forbes.com/sites/jacobmorgan/2014/10/16/why-the-collaborative-economy-is-changing-everything/#1e849e0e4fc1

12 General Electric 2016, *GE Open Innovation*, viewed 8 July 2015,
http://www.ge.com/about-us/openinnovation

For example, if automotive, oil and gas, food and construction as individual industries only hire staff, engage suppliers and interact with peer companies from within their relevant industry, what will be the outcome? The same approach, the same vein of technology. In effect, a recycling of information with limited fresh input.

Companies are doing themselves a disservice. This approach discounts the idea that other, highly progressive and capable industries could make improvements and that your business could offer the same in return.

Why are we not working closer with differing industries that are not our direct competition to see what can be done to collaborate? Why aren't oil and gas professionals sent to global food manufacturers, why can't textiles exchange staff with automotive? Why not? Alliance partnerships can be formed with no direct threat to each company, and key staff exchanged for a fixed period of time to understand what best practice looks like in another industry.

Inspiration often comes from the most unlikely of sources.

START-UPS IN EVERY BUSINESS

The business of start-ups is changing. Corporate giants are moving into the fray as organisations like Telstra and Singtel create their own start-up incubators to encourage the generation of fresh ideas.[13]

---

13 Ramli, D 2013, 'Telstra plans to incubate start-ups for $40,000 a pop', *Australian Financial Review*, 21 October, viewed 3 February 2015, http://www.afr.com/business/small-business/startup/telstra-plans-to-incubate-startups-for-40000-a-pop-20131021-jo8hr

The *Australian Financial Review* published an article in 2014 outlining the Singtel program.[14] Two hundred of its staff competed to create a start-up idea. Teams have 24 hours to develop a concept and two and a half days to build it. The three winning teams get three months off their normal job to work with an incubator firm to try and make it viable. In the end, the project belongs to the staff and Singtel will decide if it will fund it or buy it out.

Google's now famous '20 per cent time' has spawned a movement of companies, large and small, encouraging team members to work on new business ideas that are independent of their day jobs. This approach flies in the face of convention where 'moonlighting' was traditionally frowned upon. Like it or not, these activities are now a normal part of business.

According to Fast Company, increasingly employers are valuing their team having entrepreneurial skills to keep up with the constantly shifting markets.[15] What better way to develop their skills than by cutting their teeth on their own programs and bringing the benefits of that knowledge to your business? One school of thought is to put structure around the creativity, bring it into the light, remove the taboo and harness the creativity for the benefit of your business.

14 Smith, P 2014, 'Pollenizer pivots toward teaching big corporates 'start-up science', but will replenish its incubation pool', *Australian Financial Review*, 23 September, viewed 3 February 2015, http://www.afr.com/it-pro/pollenizer-pivots-toward-teaching-big-corporates-startup-science-but-will-replenish-its-incubation-pool-20140923-jyow3

15 Vanderkam, L 2014, 'Why Encouraging Employees To Be Entrepreneurs Can Create An Incredible Place To Work', *Fast Company*, 16 January, viewed 3 February 2015, http://www.fastcompany.com/3024888/work-smart/why-encouraging-employees-to-be-entrepreneurs-can-create-an-incredible-place-to-work

COMMERCIAL TIE-BACK

What is your business known for? What is your core product or service? Does it provide a complete and exceptional solution that addresses your customers' top problems? Do you have a clear process for taking a client from a state of difficulty to opportunity?

Assuming you can tick off the above, does your business have logical follow-on products? By this I mean, if your business offers remarkable solutions, your customers will be looking for other opportunities to purchase from you.

These follow-on products are for your ideal customers, the ones you love to work with and who love engaging with you. These products are the goods and services that significantly differentiate you from your competitors.

In a crowded economy, when technology and change are moving so fast, it is not enough to be seen as the authority for what you do but be a business that can provide a comprehensive solution to your customers' challenges.

For instance:

1. A health food manufacturer may offer a wellness program.

2. An agribusiness company may offer training to chefs on how to prepare their premium product.

3. A car company may offer defensive driver training.

4. A surgeon may provide lifestyle apparel to help patients recover from traumatic surgery.

5. A family law practice may supply services to help children as their parents go through divorce proceedings.

Take a look at your core products and services. What complementary next-step services can your business provide to assist your customers? Which suppliers and collaborative partners are needed to make this happen?

TOP TIPS

1. Analyse how procurement is accessing new and different ways of thinking from alternative industry sectors. Identify what your company is doing to capture and apply this knowledge.

2. Whether you sell goods or services, does your company have digital, scalable products? How could you create them?

3. Consider how your business could create additional follow-on products and services for the clients who love what you do. Review how procurement could assist in the design, build and management of these products and supply relationships.

CHAPTER 17

Are You Ready?

We live in a world that looks for immediate answers and instantaneous solutions. Before we know it, we've moved onto the next pressing need.

There's a problem with this fast paced, no-time-to-waste, next-please culture. We simply don't stop to draw breath, nor consider the benefits that come from a pause for reflection. If we are going to make genuine inroads, there must be time to test and measure. We should be considering what we've done well, what can be improved and, most importantly, how we arrived at these outcomes.

There's no better time to start than now.

A self-assessment style table has been included below. This outlines the most important concepts from each chapter, giving you the opportunity to test how your business measures up.

As a leader, if you understand the effectiveness of your company in these specific areas, you will be better equipped to direct the team with a clear course for improvement.

It's up to you.

Self-Assessed Improvement Plan

Chapter 1: A Framework for Success

Structured frameworks are vital in business. Besides taking a company's best thinking and documenting it for all to follow, structured frameworks allow the team to consistently learn and apply this knowledge. Procurement is no exception. The function needs to demonstrate high competency toward integration, flexibility, partnership, team capability and commerciality. How does procurement in your business stack up?

What are your Opportunities for Improvement?

Chapter 2: Six Common Mistakes

No matter the industry, there are a number of common procurement mistakes that businesses make. Six of the most frequent pitfalls have been listed. Which ones are made by your company and what financial gains are possible through improvement?

What are your Opportunities for Improvement?

Self-Assessed Improvement Plan

Chapter 3: It Starts From the Top

Leadership empowers leadership. A supported procurement team can generate substantially greater financial results than if left and ignored. How? Permission is given to ask the sensitive questions, challenge existing mindsets and propose progressive change without a cloud of resistance. Procurement is no different to any other function in business; it's here to contribute toward company profit and growth. The best way to see this happen is first to empower them for change.

What are your Opportunities for Improvement?

Chapter 4: Profiling Procurement

It can be a real challenge for some in business to love their 'client' more than their 'product'. But that is what is required from procurement. Business goals and stakeholder needs must always be a higher priority than procurement process. Whether it's a shift in thinking in the current team or the employment of a different type of practitioner, procurement's commercial effectiveness hinges on its ability to engage.

What are your Opportunities for Improvement?

Chapter 5: Why Bother With Rapport?

Commercial minded strategic partnerships are remarkably effective at lifting company performance. Surprisingly, not all companies value or appreciate the opportunities at hand. Procurement has a role to play. It's the traditional custodian of supplier relationship and the communicator of change to all levels in business. Leaders need to emphasise the importance of this mindset in their procurement team since success here can be the difference between program adoption or program failure, expense reduction or price escalation.

What are your Opportunities for Improvement?

Chapter 6: Customer of Choice

Every business should aim to be the preferential sale point for their key suppliers. The goal is to gain first access to innovation, technology, rare resources and favourable pricing. This is what it means to be a customer of choice. If your business is not preferred, then by default your competitors are. Not only is your business missing out, but competitors are also pulling ahead. Becoming a customer of choice is not a knee-jerk reaction. It's a deliberate and planned approach that is embraced by the company for the long term.

What are your Opportunities for Improvement?

Chapter 7: Innovation — Survive or Thrive

If business is not innovating, it's going backwards. An innovation mindset needs to be cultivated from within as it requires departmental divides to be removed and a selfless collaborative approach to be established. Many of the greatest innovation opportunities will come from the supply base. How is your business capitalising on what is available in the marketplace?

What are your Opportunities for Improvement?

Chapter 8: Beyond the Bottom Line

Where are you wanting to take your company? How are all facets of your business contributing toward this goal? When making your plans, remember that; cost will always be greater than price, the winners curse should never be under estimated and significant expense lies buried in the Purchase-to-Pay process. With awareness comes a shift in behaviour—this is when your corporate objectives will be enabled.

What are your Opportunities for Improvement?

Self-Assessed Improvement Plan

Chapter 9: Aligned for Results

The misaligned procurement function rarely delivers its full commercial potential. Careful consideration should be given to where the function reports and what will frame its targets. The closer procurement can be to satisfying the needs of its primary stakeholders, the greater the commercial success.

What are your Opportunities for Improvement?

Chapter 10: Prepare for the Unexpected

No business can remove all risk. It can and should be prepared for the unexpected. Effective crisis management is documented, addresses all significant risk, is endorsed by management, reviewed for currency and is frequently practiced and tested. Creating a plan will cost time and money; however, it pays for itself again and again in preventing damage to reputation, lost sales and restitution expense.

What are your Opportunities for Improvement?

Chapter 11: Mergers and Acquisitions

Procurement has a role to play throughout an acquisition event in both due diligence and integration. People, process, suppliers, technology are just a handful of areas that procurement can investigate to bring about greater financial return. With the advantage of working at the coalface of change, an effective and informed procurement team can be the difference between achieving or falling short of the benefits forecast.

What are your Opportunities for Improvement?

Chapter 12: Intelligent Contracting

Well-structured contracts are able to bring great value to a company. Built to address a specific business case, they are made available to all parties involved, can be easily communicated to new stakeholders and are operationalised allowing them to be practical and easy to manage. More than just a step in the process, contracts need to be instruments used to prepare, implement and manage a project.

What are your Opportunities for Improvement?

Chapter 13: Partner or Supplier

Supply Relationship Management (SRM) programs are established to create mutually beneficial commercial relationships between the buyer and seller. A well run SRM program will allow a company to secure first access to new innovation and technology, sustainably outcompete competition, uncover favourable cost and price scenarios, improve operating methods and minimise the risk to supply. Put simply, without a fit-for-purpose SRM program, your business is forfeiting unimaginable value.

What are your Opportunities for Improvement?

Chapter 14: Brand and Credibility

A company, department and individual each has a brand and a level of credibility. Brand and credibility need to be actively cultivated between colleagues, suppliers, clients and industry—it's this trust and authenticity that will encourage others to follow. The strength of a business is often determined by the calibre of its people. Develop the team, grow their influence and watch their increasing consequential ability to lift project adoption and commercial returns.

What are your Opportunities for Improvement?

Self-Assessed Improvement Plan

Chapter 15: Boom and Bust

Economic cycles play an important role in how a business operates. Irrespective of the environment a company finds itself in, there needs to be a measured approach on how business is conducted. In buoyant times, procurement should be developing mid-term strategies, tackling the high-stakes initiatives, investing in supply relationships and working closely with sales and marketing to maximise profits. In tighter periods, that same team should be investing in profit retention methods, drawing down on supplier goodwill, improving efficiencies and retaining the talent.

What are your Opportunities for Improvement?

Chapter 16: Preparing for Tomorrow

Every business needs a plan. It needs to be larger than the next electoral cycle, the next free trade agreement or economic swing. A business needs a short, mid and long-term strategy to see it through the years ahead. So much of what we do is driven by technology development and early adoption. Procurement should be across the market trends and be working closely with suppliers, development, sales and marketing to bring to life the next generation of technology that will see your business evolve again.

What are your Opportunities for Improvement?

WHERE TO FROM HERE?

VISION FOR OUR CLIENTS

Our vision is to equip clients with the tools, strategies and mindset required to develop trust and powerful commercial relationships with suppliers, employees and collaborative partners. From this position of strength, leaders in business can create lasting results—a commercial and social legacy that improves the lives of all that their business touch.

HOW SYNTHESIS GROUP CAN HELP

Is your business going through change, perhaps it's in need of review? If *Changing the Game* has pricked an awareness of areas for improvement, I'd love to hear about it.

Learn more and stay connected by accessing further resources on Synthesis Group's website. This is where you can get your hands on articles, guides and best practice.

If you'd like to discuss a topic further or understand how Synthesis Group can help, please reach out for a chat – no strings attached.

Our services include strategy programs, advice, coaching and project management. All services are built to accommodate the varying size and scale of mid-market companies. The goal is simple—help you generate fast and sustainable financial improvement.

We've designed our services to:

1. Identify short and mid-term opportunities to save money, lift profit and make operational improvements

2. Provide hands-on assistance and advice to deliver specific projects or programs

3. Operationalise strategies for sustainable growth

4. Lift competitiveness through partnerships, early access to innovation and improved products / services

Visit the Synthesis Group website for further details.

I look forward to starting the conversation.

William Pegg

www.synthesisgroup.com.au

A FEW FINAL WORDS

Thank you for taking the time to read *Changing the Game*. I hope you enjoyed the experience.

Two of my greatest passions in life are to learn and educate others. I believe it's the responsibility of every leader in business to share knowledge generously. We need to allow the next generation to stand on our shoulders and achieve things we never thought possible.

I have tried to write this book with sincerity and communicate from my perspective, what great business can look like. It's now up to you to decide what you'd like to do from here.

Whatever direction you choose to take, I encourage you to continue to learn, listen, share and engage.

Give from your heart all that you can. Consider the needs of others in your business dealings and personal life. Be generous with your time and words.

Until we speak again.

—William

ABOUT WILLIAM

William Pegg is the Director and founder of Synthesis Group.

With a university background in science, he made the switch to business at the start of his career when environmental science jobs were just not popular.

Trust and partnership. That is what was drummed into him as a graduate. Step forward 14 years, Synthesis Group is the result and is positioned as the authority on procurement for mid-sized businesses.

William has spent years in the 'engine room' of companies operating in FMCG, agribusiness, heavy industry, professional services, health care and mining. He counts himself fortunate to have had this exposure.

What was realised—the challenges faced are similar and mid-sized companies are frequently missing out.

William believes that greater commercial opportunities are available for companies by working with their key suppliers, clients and collaborative partners. For that purpose, *'Changing the Game'* was written—to help the leadership of mid-sized companies realise better performance from their procurement team.

A husband, father and keen cyclist, William calls Brisbane Australia home.

ACKNOWLEDGEMENTS

Not in my wildest dreams could I have pictured this. The joy, satisfaction, fatigue, price and privilege of writing this book. To call *Changing the Game* a project is an understatement. It has been a revealing yet rewarding experience that has at some moments pushed me to my limits. For their unwavering support and care, I thank my family.

To my wife, I simply could not have completed this book without your tireless involvement. For the long discussions, the late nights, the early mornings, the reading, re-reading, critique, and support. Thank you. I love you and am blessed to have you by my side.

To my children, you are both wonderful individuals and I know you will achieve great things. Never give up, never lose faith, never stop growing—you have an incredibly bright future ahead.

There have been many who have contributed in one way or another to the 'creation' process. I only hope I've mentioned them all.

John Harney, we need more people in this profession like you. Neil Rainy, your willingness to share knowledge and make introductions been invaluable. Visna Lampasi, for the years of endorsement, support, and direction—thank you. Catherine Thompson, your sharp mind and contrarian approach brought clarity—thank you. Sara Cullen, you helped the penny drop—your work is just brilliant. Bruce Beeren, thank you for helping with this project. There is much that can be learnt from you. Martin Burgman, you have always been so willing to help. Richard Savva, you've been there from the beginning.

Your support and input have been recognised and appreciated. Dhaval Buch, your willingness to share big business strategy has been powerful. Ben Evers-Swindell, you've always been in my corner. Guy Haslehurst, for a man who has the most impressive work ethic I'm grateful for your contribution. Warren Kalinko—thank you for making the complex simple. Nigel Wardropper, a huge thank you for all the introductions. Darren Bryan, I appreciate your willingness to help. Peter Turner, who would have thought a breakfast meeting could deliver so much, your input has been of immense value. Andrew Reeson, the future looks bright, I thoroughly enjoyed hearing your insights. Cynthia Dearin, 'keep going' has been our mantra, it's always appreciated. Van Shore, the ice is melting—thank you, my friend. And to Gary Rutherford, it all started with you!

A huge vote of thanks to Jakob Paartalu, Guy Haslehurst, Andrew Dillon, Ben Whitaker and Peter Turner for the manuscript critique. Look how far we've come. Thanks for your encouragement and enthusiasm.

Rob Holden. I had steeled myself for the editing journey. Your insight, professionalism and cut-through have changed the game. Thank you.

AND

Andrew Griffiths. You had to go and make it look so easy! Without your guidance, this project would never have seen the light of day. For that, I'm grateful more than you know.